Kenneth Weisbrode

Central Eurasia: Prize or Quicksand?

Contending views of instability in Karabakh, Ferghana and Afghanistan

Adelphi Paper **338**

Oxford University Press, Great Clarendon Street, Oxford OX2 6DP
Oxford New York
Athens Auckland Bangkok Bombay Calcutta Cape Town
Dar es Salaam Delhi Florence Hong Kong Istanbul Karachi
Kuala Lumpur Madras Madrid Melbourne Mexico City
Nairobi Paris Singapore Taipei Tokyo Toronto
and associated companies in
Berlin Ibadan

Oxford is a trade mark of Oxford University Press

Published in the United States
by Oxford University Press Inc., New York

© The International Institute for Strategic Studies 2001

First published May 2001 by **Oxford University Press** for
The International Institute for Strategic Studies
Arundel House, 13–15 Arundel Street, Temple Place, London WC2R 3DX
www.iiss.org

Director John Chipman
Editor Mats R. Berdal
Project Manager, Design and Production Mark Taylor

British Library Cataloguing in Publication Data
Data available

Library of Congress Cataloguing in Publication Data

ISBN 0-19-851070-5
ISSN 0567-932x

Contents

Maps

Introduction

Contrary to widespread expectations, the dissolution of the Soviet Union did not plunge Central Eurasia into immediate turmoil. But a decade later, stability in the region is eroding rapidly. Basic economic conditions have deteriorated in each of the newly-independent states of the South Caucasus and Central Asia; most of their institutions and nearly all of their governments are weak or failing; and terrorism is on the rise. This paper takes a fresh look at the strategic significance of a region that is still unfamiliar to many people outside its borders. Are its problems merely the stubborn residue of empire, to be overcome in time? Or has a longer-term phenomenon set in? If so, does this constitute a danger that should worry outsiders, particularly in the West?

The region's future seemed much rosier during the mid-1990s. Then, the policies of most Western countries, particularly the US, were based on the premise that, despite their problems, the majority of Central Eurasian countries were generally stable, and could be influenced in ways that would consolidate their independence and promote their economic development.[1] Yet the region's nine states – Armenia, Azerbaijan, Georgia, Kazakstan, Kyrgyzstan, Tajikistan, Turkmenistan, Uzbekistan and Afghanistan – remain poor and remote from the developed world. Economic and political reform has been slow, and no country seems able to engage in regional diplomacy that does not appear aimed at thwarting another's stated goals.

This paper identifies three areas in particular which have given grounds for deep concern: Karabakh, the Ferghana valley and Afghanistan. These conflicts are serious in themselves. But they also demonstrate how regional instability encourages outside powers to promote policies whose chief goal has been combating the influence of perceived 'enemies'. The case of Karabakh illustrates how rivalries in the South Caucasus have prevented Iran, Russia and Turkey from helping Armenia and Azerbaijan to emerge from war and poverty, and precluded the US from playing a neutral role in the region's affairs. The case of the Ferghana valley demonstrates how the combination of local insurgencies and tension between Uzbekistan and its neighbours has drawn Russia, China, the US and possibly Iran into unwitting involvement in what has already begun to resemble a quagmire. And the Afghan conflict has strained relations between Iran and Pakistan and Russia and Pakistan, with repercussions for India, the Gulf states and the West.

All three cases also highlight the conflicting views of the region's importance among the major powers, and the drawbacks of an infatuation with outdated 'chessboard' models of international relations, whose popularity after the Cold War has been resurrected by a handful of influential, mainly American, strategists. Their views of this region remain faithful to Sir Halford Mackinder's 'heartland' thesis, which assigned Eurasia a pivotal role in the global balance of power.[2] This proposition, elaborated nearly a century ago, still resonates among strategists who equate international relations with great-power politics. For them, the 'Eurasian balance of power' determines relative positions in a global hierarchy of strong and weak states, constantly in competition for advantage over one another and for leverage over smaller states. In the words of the school's most prolific American proponent, Zbigniew Brzezinski: 'preponderance over the entire Eurasian continent serv[es] as the central basis for global primacy'.[3] Coming from a citizen of the most powerful country in the world, a plea for Eurasian preponderance sounds very much like a dressed-up claim to keep other states weak and divided – in other words, a prize for some to win and others to lose. For Brzezinski, the opponent is usually Russia; others have named China, Iran, India, Japan, Turkey, the European Union (EU) or the 'Arab World'. Thus balance of power, a sound geopolitical principle, has lost credibility since the Cold War through the translation of national prejudices into strategic imperatives.

The relevance of geopolitical gamesmanship to Central Eurasia derives in large part from its intellectual hold in the US, and the ambivalent US policies that result from it. Although most American officials dismiss the small Central Eurasian states as marginal to Western security, they have not generally abandoned the entrenched view that the US must counter or 'balance' the influence in the region of potentially hostile powers, namely Russia and Iran.[4] This dictates promoting policies in specific areas, such as energy-export routes, that benefit other powers deemed friendly to the US, like Turkey. It also means trying to entice the small regional states into cooperative relationships with each other.

By the end of the 1990s, it had become clear that the first goal undermined the second. Although Western efforts to improve relations with the region have often sprung from the widespread inclination in the US and Europe to help the newly-independent states in the spirit of post-Cold War cooperation, these efforts are largely viewed in the region as deliberate attempts to draw as much of it as possible into an American orbit. Local actors, particularly in the smaller states, tend to take geopolitical competition seriously; centuries of war and invasion have instilled a conviction that no small state is safe without a larger protector. This conviction has been expressed in numerous declarations of 'strategic partnership' with the US or Russia (or both), but these have only served to heighten mistrust among regional rivals. As a result, a decade has been wasted in sorting out imaginary rivalries, rather than erecting solid foundations for peace and development.

Applying neat geopolitical formulae to Central Eurasia is futile, and could be dangerous. This paper seeks to present a more subtle and balanced portrait of the region's strategic significance. It draws lessons from the actual behaviour and interaction of specific national and sub-national actors, instead of speculating over rivalries between faceless and monolithic states. The misplaced belief among US, Russian and other analysts in the central importance of geopolitical rivalry represents a cumulative failure of imagination. In each of the major powers, analysts and policy-makers have failed to understand or respect other states' legitimate objectives, especially in intersecting borderlands.

The three cases that follow – Karabakh, the Ferghana valley and Afghanistan – also illustrate how difficult it is for outside powers and regional states to identify common strategic priorities, even when a majority both outside and within the region are faced with similar enemies. The governments of China, Iran, Russia, the US and Turkey have all identified Sunni radicalism and the international spread of narcotics and terrorism from this region as prime threats. Yet their adherence to chessboard determinism has made it extremely difficult for them to cooperate with regional states in dealing with these threats. Whether this remains the case depends as much on how governments go about identifying their countries' priorities, as on whether instability worsens. Nominal cooperation may indeed continue, but so too will perceived rivalries, with greater risks for all involved.

This failure of understanding and cooperation raises wider questions about the creation and manipulation of 'client states' in the contemporary world. This is especially important for US policy-makers. The US took the lead in seeking new 'partnerships' in Central Eurasia in the 1990s, partnerships which influential American analysts did not hesitate to portray in traditional client-state terms. There were suggestions, for instance, that the US should help the Karimov regime in Uzbekistan to become a kind of 'regional policeman', a role akin to that played in the 1960s and 1970s by the Shah's Iran. Yet simultaneously, American representatives claimed that the US opposed on principle traditional sphere-of-influence behaviour, preferring instead a new and equal democratic order. The evident contradictions in this approach greatly increased the suspicions of Russia and Iran, and encouraged an equally 'geo-political' reaction by both powers. These unanalysed contradictions contributed a damaging level of unclear thinking about Central Eurasia in past US administrations. A key aim of this paper is to bring more clarity to this thinking.

Chapter 1

A 'New' Area on the Map

What is Central Eurasia?

The Central Eurasian region stretches from the Bosphorus in the west to the eastern borders of the Chinese province of Xinjiang, and from the Kazak steppe in the north to the Indian Ocean in the south. Most policy-makers, particularly in the West, have sought to divide the area into clearly-distinguishable parts. Immediately following the collapse of the Soviet Union, there was a tendency to consider the region narrowly as the southern tier of the former empire, which post-Soviet Russia has termed the 'near abroad'. This definition supported the widespread view in both the former Soviet Union and the West that the former Soviet territories were linked by some common factor, and that most geopolitical issues in the region could be reduced to either favouring or opposing Russian hegemony. Within this regional concept existed an older sub-division that made use of the most obvious geographic boundary – the Caspian Sea – to bisect the region into the South Caucasus, comprising the three former Soviet states of Armenia, Azerbaijan and Georgia; and Central Asia, comprising the five republics east of the Caspian – Kazakstan, Kyrgyzstan, Tajikistan, Turkmenistan and Uzbekistan.

These definitions are oversimplifications for two reasons. Firstly, the emphasis on the old Soviet borders not only promotes the fiction that the Commonwealth of Independent States (CIS) is the most potent force in the region's affairs, but also excludes territories with important historic, ethnic and cultural ties to Central Eurasia. These territories include Afghanistan, northern Iran, the northern

Map 1 Central Eurasia

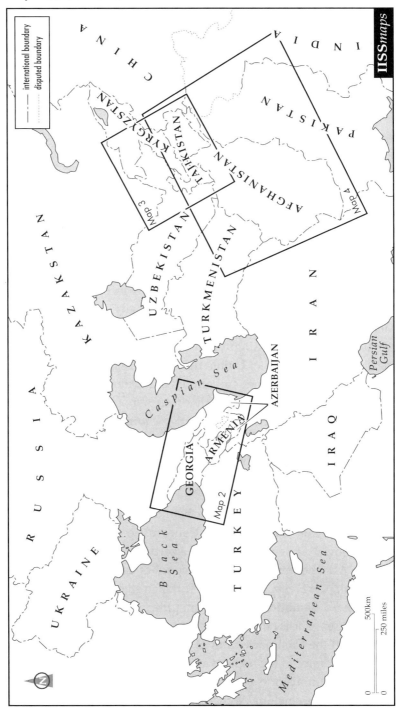

Caucasus, north-western China, Kashmir and the Tibetan plateau. With most of the region now either independent or aspiring to be so, defining it by one particular imperial standard rather than by historical and cultural associations obscures the variety of alliance patterns that may yet emerge.

Secondly, drawing a line down the middle of the Caspian and asserting the geopolitical separation of the Caucasus from Central Asia suggests an east–west division that belies the economic and political links between the two territories, notably in the area of hydrocarbons. The trans-Caspian division may be meaningful for China or India, which have far more reason to be concerned about events on their borders than in the faraway Caucasus, but makes less sense for Russia or Iran, which border both sides of the divide, or for Europe or the US, which border neither.

In resisting intra-regional distinctions, this paper does not discount the numerous local differences, nor does it suggest that the region is politically or culturally homogeneous. The extent of these differences, particularly between the South Caucasus and Central Asia, means that Central Eurasia obviously does not conform to the traditional notion of an integrated region.[1] Its multiple internal contrasts and layers of imperial legacy mean that Central Eurasia is interactive, not integrative. There is no cohesive or powerful post-Soviet order; indeed, the region's principal feature is its lack of both order and precision.[2]

The danger of defining the region too narrowly is that this can lead to political rigidities or artificial priorities. For example, the Pentagon places the Caucasus under the remit of the US Commander-in-Chief for Europe (who is also NATO's Supreme Allied Commander-Europe) and assigns the five Central Asian states to US Central Command, whose primary responsibility is the Middle East. This makes a strong statement to regional leaders about where their countries fit into the world-view of powerful outsiders.

To make strategic sense of the enormous expanse of territory that connects Asia with Europe, geographic inclusion is therefore more useful than exclusion.[3] The countries on one side of the Caspian, the Taklamakan desert or the Hindu Kush differ greatly from those on the other. However, just as Mexico and Canada may be discussed in the context of North America, or as Spain and Norway are categorised as parts of Western Europe, the states of both Central Asia and the Caucasus should be considered within a broader regional framework.

Which Are the Major Powers?

To assess Central Eurasia's future, it is essential to understand the perceptions and roles of the different actors – regional states and major powers. In this paper, regional states are the eight former Soviet states listed above, together with Afghanistan. The major powers are those countries bordering the region, and with substantial interests in it, namely China, India, Iran, Pakistan, Russia and Turkey, as well as the US, whose status as a global power links it to developments there. (The EU and the developed economies of East Asia – Japan and South Korea – lack common borders with the region, and their interests there are only marginal.) A power is defined as 'major' for the purposes of this paper if its relations with the region are characterised by two qualities:

- they involve a number of different regional states, through common borders or through ethnic affinities; and
- the size, wealth or geopolitical position of the power in question enables it to exercise substantially more influence over regional states than they can reciprocate.[4]

Most officials, both in major powers and in regional states, seem to understand that the origins of the region's problems are internal, and internal solutions must be found. Yet they have been less successful in interpreting each other's diplomatic 'body language', complicating both the problems, and the solutions. Hence, the impressions regional leaders and their counterparts in Moscow, Washington, Ankara, Tehran, Islamabad and Beijing have formed of each other's interests have been as important as the interests themselves.

Moreover, many official positions with regard to national interests in this region have been superficial and fluctuating. National consensus is hard to identify as each major power harbours a variety of constituencies contending for influence. In Russia, there are conflicting views of what the country's posture towards the newly-independent states should be. The military, the foreign ministry and the energy industry all differ over the degree of direct influence the Russian state and private actors should exert in Central Eurasia. In Turkey, the foreign ministry and the armed forces share the view that Turkey should keep a low profile east of the Caspian, but they must contend with the greater ambitions of politicians and private groups, notably educational and religious organisations, which want Turkey to exert greater influence abroad. Opinions are also divided in China and Iran, whose national oil companies have become important geopolitical actors in their own right. Pakistan's volatile politics hinge not only on issues like corruption and the state of the economy, but also on the role of Islamic groups, both internally and in Afghanistan and Kashmir. Finally, US policy towards Central Eurasia has been disputed among competing lobbies and pressure groups within and outside the official bureaucracy.

Impressions and Policies

The policies of most governments in the region have been ambivalent and unsettled. This was initially because the Soviet collapse caught almost everyone by surprise. As its inevitability became clear, most local leaderships tried to adapt as best they could. Nationalists in the Caucasus, like Georgia's Zviad Gam-sakhurdia or Azerbaijan's Abulfez Elchibey, assumed power, only to be replaced by prominent former members of the Soviet élite, who adopted much of their opponents' nationalist platform. In all the Central Asian republics apart from Kyrgyzstan, pre-disintegration leaders held on to power, but here too all sought to reinvent themselves as nationalists.[5]

Nationalism found expression in five ways:

* the replacement of consensual reciprocity among local leaderships with centralised executive power;
* more pronounced hostility towards regional neighbours;
* the promotion of historic and cultural symbols;
* the diversification of foreign relations, manifest through aggressive efforts to achieve a higher profile in world affairs; and
* an ambivalent or actively hostile attitude towards Russia.

All five elements provided the framework for developing relations with Russia, and the other major powers.

Relations with Russia

The nature of relations with Moscow has varied among the regional states. Azerbaijan and Uzbekistan appeared to want to distance themselves, securing the exit of Russian troops from their soil and enjoying honeymoons with the West from around 1994 until 1998. In Uzbekistan's case, this was because the state was stronger than its neighbours, lacked borders with Russia and had regional ambitions of its own. For Azerbaijan, the main factors were its historic ties with both Turkey and Iran, its key position at the western gateway to the Caspian Sea and its promising future as an abundant source of hydrocarbons and transit point for trade.

By contrast, civil wars and proximity to the volatile northern Caucasus forced Georgia to accept a continued Russian military presence, while doing its best to achieve full independence. Georgia's leader, former Soviet Foreign Minister Eduard Shevard-nadze, complained about Russian pressure on his regime and the presence of Russian troops on Georgian territory, although Soviet troops provided arms to the December 1991 rebellion against Gamsakhurdia which eventually brought Shevardnadze to power, and also gave him critical help against a rebellion in October 1993. In Armenia, Kyrgyzstan and Tajikistan, inclination towards Russia had more to do with economic dependence, sentimental links or the presumption that Russia was still the only protector – of the Kyrgyz and Tajiks against the Uzbeks; of the Armenians against the Azeris and Turks; and of the Georgians and Abkhaz against one another. Even so, Kyrgyz President Askar Akaev secured his country's entry into the World Trade Organisation (WTO) in 1998, the first post-Soviet state to do so, in the face of Russian opposition and the Kyrgyz economy's almost total dependence on Russia. Kazakstan, because of its large Russian population, long border with Russia and dependence on Russian outlets for its energy, has had little choice but to maintain good relations with Moscow. Turkmenistan's leader Saparmurad Niyazov has been alone in the region in proclaiming a strictly neutral policy for his country, refusing to participate fully in the activities of the CIS or NATO's Partnership for Peace (PfP), while assuring his neighbours that Turkmen neutrality would in practice enhance friendly relations with them. However, Turkmen policy, particularly on energy, was realigned decisively towards Russia by the end of the 1990s.

In Russia, there are also conflicting views on what the country's posture towards the newly-independent states should be. Russian foreign policy from the early to mid-1990s was oriented towards Europe and, with the exceptions of the wars in Chechnya and occasional interventions in Tajikistan and elsewhere, was relatively disengaged from the 'near abroad'. This choice did not mark a dramatic change; Russian/Soviet imperial traditions have ranged from benign to aggressive since the nineteenth-century conquest of these territories.[6] Former President Boris Yeltsin, whose brand of nationalism was more opportunist than expansionist, appeared to want little to do with these states, and only condemned outside 'interference' in both the Caucasus and Central Asia after the 1995 war in Chechnya. Notwithstanding the 'Primakov doctrine' (named after Yevgeniy Primakov, Russian foreign minister from 1996 to 1998) of strengthening Russia's hold over the 'near abroad' and opposing the influence of outsiders, namely the US and Turkey, the viability of the CIS was never taken seriously under Yeltsin.

Towards the end of the 1990s, however, Russia's stratified view of national security, which placed priority on some regions over others, appeared to give way to something closer to a maximalist approach that required the stabilisation of all frontiers.[7] Thus, it was important to reaffirm Russia's strength, particularly along its southern border, which many Russians still see as extending to the outer perimeter of the CIS. At the end of 1999, Russia released a new defence doctrine calling for stronger defence relationships among the former Soviet states, as well as substantial increases in defence expenditure. At the January 2000 CIS summit, new President Vladimir Putin made a strong case for reinvigorating the confederation apparatus in a bid to combat terrorism. Unlike in previous summits, his fellow CIS leaders accepted this implied increase in Russia's involvement in their affairs. Even Uzbekistan's outspokenly independent leader, Islam Karimov, supported Putin's anti-terrorist message, and sought to strengthen Uzbekistan's December 1999 *rapprochement* with Russia in the wake of growing fears of Islamic militancy. In the weeks following the summit, similar doctrines were issued by Kazakstan, Kyrgyzstan and Uzbekistan.[8] The following May, Putin visited Turkmenistan and Uzbekistan, his first foreign tour after his inauguration, and in January 2001 he travelled to Azerbaijan. By this time, attempts to forge renewed ties with the Central Eurasian region as a whole through the CIS had given way to efforts to negotiate a range of bilateral agreements.

The fluctuations in its approach to the CIS suggest that Russia's policy towards the 'near abroad' is more complicated than a simple quest for hegemony. Early twentieth-century concepts of heartland, pivot and rimland have undergone something of a renaissance in Russia since the mid-1990s, just as they have enjoyed a new vogue among Western thinkers like Brzezinski, who argue strongly in favour of forward policies on the part of Western and Asian states in order to limit Russian power.[9] Each side in the argument admits that Russia's extensive land borders and history of invasion dictate a general Russian preference for leverage or outright control over neighbouring countries, rather than an opening up of regional economic and political relationships. But the lengths Russia will go to obstruct such opening remain unclear. Also unclear is whether Russian strategists still consider it more important to concentrate power to the west than to do so to the south. A realignment from south to west was seen a century ago, when defeat in the war with Japan and the emerging German threat brought about accommodation with Britain. At present, with Russia facing actual or perceived threats from both Islamic radicalism and NATO expansion, Moscow's strategic dilemma is much more complicated, if less menacing.

The Limits to Courtship

The pro-Russian stance of most regional states at the end of the 1990s was as much due to their lack of alternative allies as it was the result of any innate sympathy with Russia, or out of mere habit. The regional states' attempts to court the West – particularly the US – did not bring the anticipated benefits, while US preoccupations with human rights complicated the already difficult implementation of what officials in states like Azerbaijan, Kazakstan and Uzbekistan imagined to be embryonic client relationships. Nor were the Turkish and Iranian governments more forthcoming with patronage given their lack of resources, inherent caution towards involvement in Central Eurasia and more pressing priorities elsewhere. The anticipated struggle between Turkey and Iran for moral leadership of the region's Muslims never took place, and neither power's purported regional mission proved well suited to the wishes of Muslims, devout or otherwise, in the Caucasus and Central Asia. For China and India, their notional status as emerging world powers was not strong enough to overcome their lack of familiarity with Central Asian problems, or the widespread prejudice in the region against allowing either power influence over its affairs.

Regional governments have nonetheless tried to curry favour with new patrons – Armenia and Turkmenistan with Iran; Azerbaijan with Turkey; and Kazakstan and Kyrgyzstan with China. But this has achieved little beyond open-ended promises of goodwill and token investments. Total foreign direct investment in the eight former Soviet states in 1999 amounted to some $2.5 billion, although there had been plans for more than ten times as much. Central Eurasia's trade with the rest of the world declined by about 40% between 1997 and 1999.[10]

More relevant to stability than these macroeconomic indicators is the region's related socio-economic decline. Since 1997, life expectancy, literacy and fertility rates and nutrition levels have fallen in nearly every country in the region. In Tajikistan, struggling to recover from war damage amounting to some $7bn, the average salary is about $10 a month. The infant mortality rate is 32 per 1,000 births, and rising.[11] The country, along with most of the region, faced the worst drought in 30 years in late 1999 and 2000. In Armenia, literacy rates have fallen by an annual 4–5% since 1997, while the fertility rate in Uzbekistan dropped by 9% in 1998. Population growth in Kyrgyzstan fell by 31% in 1999, in Armenia by 25% in 1998, and in Afghanistan by an average of 15% a year. Levels of internal migration are high: an estimated four million people have moved from one part of the region to another during the past ten years.

Given these grim conditions, neighbouring powers as well as the US have approached the region with considerable caution. As the 1990s progressed, they were inclined to see it as an extension of

Afghanistan – described by one Indian expert as 'the perpetual vortex of a storm that spews forth all manner of evil' – as against the earlier Western view of a giant 'strategic vacuum' destined to be filled.[12] The growing problem of international terrorism, identified with Afghanistan and more broadly with radical Sunni (and to a much lesser extent Shi'a) Islam, has driven all the major powers apart from Pakistan into what might be presumed to be a community of interest. However, their ability to cooperate against the perceived threat lacked a more accurate understanding of the underlying factors giving rise to terrorism. But above all else, a convergence of interests among the major powers could not occur in the absence of a common understanding of the region as a whole, and of what each power desired from it.

All of the major powers with interests in Central Eurasia regard maintaining stability there as the most important issue. Although they differ over how stability is to be promoted, all have preferred to try to contain or manage the principal threats rather than intervene directly – with the exception of Russian and Uzbek participation in the Tajik civil war of the 1990s, and the continued Russian troop presence in Tajikistan. But by the end of the decade, this policy of non-intervention was allowing the problems of Central Eurasia to deteriorate to the point of becoming destabilising in themselves. Regional governments could not resolve conflicts on their own, while the major powers were not interested in moving beyond what Lord Curzon, in reference to Russia, once called 'a hand-to-mouth policy … of waiting upon events, or by profiting by the blunders of others, and as often of committing the like herself'.

The East and the South

Geography imposes its own rules, often against the wishes of states. Neither Russia nor the other major neighbouring powers can at once contain and remain aloof from the region's problems. Regional leaders, by contrast, tend to emphasise inter-connection; Boris Shikhmuradov, the former foreign minister of Turkmenistan, once noted that the foreign relations of his country and its neighbours could be summarised in the history of contact between the Persian and Russian empires.[13] Throughout history, Central Eurasia has been fought over – by Slavs, Mongols, Turks, Persians and Arabs. Today's

– albeit mostly peaceful – competition over pipeline routes, political alliances and religious affiliations marks the latest chapter in this perennial struggle, in which each group has sought to maximise its leverage through alliances with more powerful collaborators. How relevant today is this frame of mind? And how does it relate to the interests of potential allies besides Russia and the West?

China

In the former Soviet states of Central Asia, China is widely perceived as an ambitious power, a feared source of human and manufactured exports and, given its record in Xinjiang and Tibet, a ruthless actor in its dealings with local populations in its path. However, China's involvement in what used to be known as Turkestan has been defensive: controlling those 'inside the wall', and preventing outsiders from crossing over.[14] Beijing has based its approach to regional affairs on internal preoccupations, rather than perceptions of other powers' ambitions, or a presumption that their gains must come at China's expense. This could change if relations with India worsen, or if the China–Pakistan relationship deteriorates. Nonetheless, Pacific-oriented China has a weaker and more intermittent presence west of the Tien Shan than any major power apart from the US and the EU. Compared with Iran, Russia, Turkey or the South Asian states, it has little recent history of involvement with Central Asia, and even less with the Caucasus.

India

In contrast to regional perceptions of China, India is rarely seen as having ambitions in the region, given its history of invasion from the north and its more recent record of deference to Soviet interests. But India also has a long history of northward migration. Indian (Hindustani) communities flourished throughout Central Asia from the fourteenth to the nineteenth centuries, and existed in Afghanistan until the end of the twentieth. While it is doubtful that Indian traders are potential agents of Indian geopolitical influence or harbingers of some future drive for *Lebensraum*, many Indians, particularly Muslims, consider themselves Central Eurasians, and will increasingly seek to become involved directly in the region's affairs.

Pakistan

Pakistan has played an aggressive role in the Afghan conflict since the early 1980s. Pakistani supporters of this involvement contend that it is defensive, dictated by their country's isolation and in any case indistinguishable from similar involvement in Afghanistan by India, Iran and Russia. In this view, Pakistan's enemies will waste little time in further dismembering the country unless its leaders pursue aggressive forward policies in Afghanistan, Kashmir, Iranian Baluchistan and elsewhere.[15] Islamabad is also convinced that foreign adventurism mitigates, rather than worsens, sectarian strife at home. At a more fundamental level, the spectre of an Afghan–Indian alliance, an important factor in Pakistan's strategic thinking from the 1950s to the 1970s, continues to haunt its policy-makers, however remote such a development might be.

Iran

Central Eurasia's avowedly secular regimes initially viewed Iran as the chief source of anti-secularism in the region – a view strongly shared by the US. However, Tehran has been one of the main opponents of Sunni radical missionary activity, both because its proponents have been backed by Iran's regional rivals in Kabul and Islamabad, and because of enduring Shi'a–Sunni hostility. Like Pakistan, however, Iran's relations with its neighbours are dictated more by its sense of geographic vulnerability than by religious ambition. Tehran sees itself as surrounded by states and cultures – Azeri, Turkmen, Uzbek, Iraqi and Pushtun – which are either non-Persian, or non-Shi'a. Azeri nationalism in particular poses a major potential threat to the unity of the Iranian state. As a result, Iran's closest allies in Central Eurasia have been Christian Armenia and Russia. Another concern Iranian leaders may have in the region is that if peace is finally achieved in the Middle East, those in Israel and the West who advocate marginalising Iran may centre their activities on the country's vulnerable northern and eastern borders.[16]

The American Energy Catalyst

Until 1994, Central Eurasia was of little interest in the US beyond a small community of specialists. Although there were Cold War attempts to arouse greater interest, these focused on the region as a potentially vulnerable flank of the Soviet empire. Soon after the Central Eurasian states gained independence, US Secretary of State James Baker visited the region and opened the first US embassies there. Thought was initially given to extending US influence to combat the possible emergence of Iranian-style Islamic regimes but when these did not appear, interest in Central Asia waned, although the Caucasus continued to attract American attention because of the war in Karabakh, and Shevardnadze's residual popularity.

The marginal status of these countries was in line with the policy adopted by Bill Clinton's administration on taking office in 1992. This regarded amicable relations with Russia as a priority, and viewed overtures towards these states as a distraction or, worse, a provocation to Moscow. Clinton's leading adviser on Russia, Strobe Talbott (later to become Deputy Secretary of State), was adamant that strong US support for the Yeltsin regime was essential to prevent the return of communism.[17] The Department of Defense was also eager to secure Russian cooperation in areas such as nuclear non-proliferation. Bureaucrats were directed to avoid criticising any aspect of this 'Russia-first' policy, an instruction soon extended to cover most Russian actions within its borders.

By mid-1994, however, the region's energy potential – estimated then at over 200bn barrels of oil – had begun to attract renewed interest, and the 'Caspian region' enjoyed a remarkable vogue among a small, vocal group of policy-makers.[18] By the middle of the decade, there were conferences on the Caspian in Washington almost every week, new institutes were founded to study Central Eurasian history and politics, and bilateral business councils created for every country in the region. Cabinet secretaries and members of Congress made numerous visits; in Baku and Tashkent in particular, expectations rose to the point of envisaging special relationships with the Americans comparable to those between the US and Saudi Arabia or Iran under the Shah. The US also initiated a series of military exchanges and joint exercises, culminating in the September 1997 parachute drop by the 82nd Airborne Division along with Russian, Turkish, Kazak, Kyrgyz and Uzbek soldiers onto a remote part of the southern Kazak steppe. By 1999, both Azerbaijan and Georgia had invited NATO to establish bases on their territory as a prelude to membership, while Uzbekistan, Kazakstan and

Kyrgyzstan all sought to promote themselves as the 'strategic pillar' of the US in Central Asia.

By 1997, a new Caspian inter-agency group had been established at the National Security Council (NSC), and the president had named a special adviser on Caspian issues. A self-sustaining bureaucratic constituency had formed, with members in the Office of the Secretary of Defense and in the departments of Commerce, Energy and State. The leading officials involved – Sheila Heslin from the NSC, Federico Peña and later Bill Richardson at the Department of Energy, and Jan Kalicki at the Department of Commerce – finally settled on an organising, strategic principle: a 'New Silk Road'. This foresaw a 'corridor' of prosperous, stable and secular states more-or-less allied with Western interests and providing a balance to what were considered to be Russian, Iranian or Chinese regional ambitions. In 1998, Congress first introduced a 'Silk Road Strategy Act' to establish multiple pipelines to bring Kazak, Turkmen and Azeri oil and gas to market. By now, energy reserves in and around the Caspian were estimated at 100bn barrels of oil and about 200 trillion cubic feet of natural gas.[19]

Russia controlled existing export routes, while potential ones through Iran were considered to be the most commercially efficient and profitable. The multiple-pipelines policy was thus aimed at preventing either Tehran or Moscow from monopolising access to the region's energy reserves.[20] The US, with Turkey, began to promote an alternative route from Baku in Azerbaijan across Georgia to the Turkish Mediterranean port of Ceyhan. This pipeline, which has been on the drawing board for over five years, is estimated to be far more expensive than any alternative, but has the advantage of bypassing the congested and environmentally precarious Bosphorus. It is also one of the few routes to skirt Iran and Russia. Others are the Baku–Supsa pipeline, which also passes through Georgia; a set of proposed – and since shelved – lines from Turkmenistan through Afghanistan to Pakistan; and the most ambitious and costly project of all, a pipeline from Kazakstan to China, which is also still in the planning stages.

The Baku–Ceyhan route was a deliberate attempt to enhance Turkish prestige, an effort to satisfy the hopes of regional states for a US commitment to safeguard their independence, and a bid to preempt charges by some American lobbies that the US was not doing enough to steer the region away from excessive Iranian or Russian influence. The considerable time, effort and prestige invested in the scheme meant that several US officials, notably Richardson and Kalicki, and Special Caspian Advisers Richard Morningstar and John Wolf, were reluctant to abandon it despite vocal opposition, not least from the large multinational oil companies, which favoured shorter, cheaper routes, mainly through Iran.[21]

The diplomatic costs have been high. The plans heralded a split with European policies towards the region, which are less geared to either excluding Iran or promoting Turkey's leverage over regional energy markets.[22] They were also at variance with the official policy of improving relations with Iran and Russia. Both Tehran and Moscow are strongly opposed to the pipeline, and have advanced explicitly anti-Western views, combining historic mistrust and fear of Turkish influence with a more recently-acquired resentment of American power.[23] As a result, both countries have found it difficult to respond seriously to US promises of good faith in other areas.

The political pursuit of such an ambitious development scheme in the absence of a viable framework for regional co-operation dealt a blow to US and other Western efforts to play a neutral and constructive role in Central Eurasian affairs. Not only did it violate the maxim that good diplomacy is three-quarters' presentation, but it also put a narrow, competitive agenda, based on mercantile advantage, at odds with a confused mixture of commercial, political and strategic aims. Given the omnipotent image of the US, it is easy to overestimate its effect on regional situations. Nonetheless, its competitive approach towards the other powers had a crucial symbolic impact, exacerbating latent rivalries in the region and reinforcing a general perception of antagonism.

In the course of 2000, it began to seem that the long-delayed Baku–Ceyhan project might become practicable, thanks to a shift in the attitude of the leading oil companies. This was not, however, the result of stronger US support or a changed geopolitical configuration, but of two purely commercial developments: the considerably higher international price of crude oil, and the discovery of a major new oilfield off the coast of Kazakstan.

Nonetheless, the major oil companies remain cautious, particularly in view of the looming succession issue in Azerbaijan. Moreover, most of the new Kazak fields will take a decade or more to come on stream. As Ed Chow, a former senior executive with Chevron and Special Adviser to the Georgian government, has emphasised, 'Anyone impatient for Baku–Ceyhan does not understand the history of the oil industry'.[24]

Forging a New Pecking Order

No regional government in Central Eurasia considers its prestige and the pursuit of its interests without taking into account what it assesses to be the ambitions of the US, Russia, Iran, Turkey and other major powers. Within the region itself, the psychology of competition was mirrored in the ambitions of local authorities. Regimes in each country have sought to bolster state power by winning outside backing, thereby combining their desires to maintain tight control at home, deter outside intervention and, ultimately, fix in place a regional hierarchy. But while no government has achieved the internal stability necessary to support its rhetoric of regional superiority, each has succeeded in making neighbours nervous. Political concerns have often echoed cultural stereotypes. Azerbaijan is perceived by many Armenians, Russians and Iranians to be an agent of Turkish ambition in the Caucasus. Uzbekistan is almost universally seen by its neighbours as a reckless hegemon in the making, potentially backed by the US. Besides fostering precisely the conditions of insecurity that the quest for external support was intended to preclude, these perceptions complicated what was already bound to be a difficult process of post-imperial adjustment. The future does not, therefore, look promising for the states and people of Central Eurasia.

Chapter 2

Karabakh and the South Caucasus

The dispute between Armenia and Azerbaijan over Karabakh has been the most protracted to emerge on the territory of the former Soviet Union.[1] It affects an area contiguous to Iran and Turkey, and provides a good illustration of how these states, along with Russia, have perceived their interests in the South Caucasus, and acted in respect of them. All three have been involved, together with the US, as mediators and protagonists. Important domestic constituencies in the major powers have also been implicated, particularly Armenia's backers in the US, France and Russia, and Azerbaijan's supporters in Turkey and, to a lesser extent, in the US. The conflict is also relevant to formal or quasi-formal security agreements between major powers and rival states in the region. In these respects, the Karabakh dispute is less like other protracted conflicts in the Caucasus, such as those over Abkhazia, Chechnya and Ossetia, and more like the international disputes that have emerged east of the Caspian.

Background

The war over Karabakh began in 1988 and reached a climax in 1992–93, before a cease-fire was signed in May 1994. Its origins lie at least as far back as the Soviet decision in 1923 to make Nagorno-Karabakh, although largely populated by Armenians, an Autonomous Oblast within Azerbaijan (partly in an effort to maintain good relations with Atatürk's Turkey). This separated Karabakh's Armenians from the Armenian Soviet Socialist Republic, and made

Map 2 Karabakh and the South Caucasus

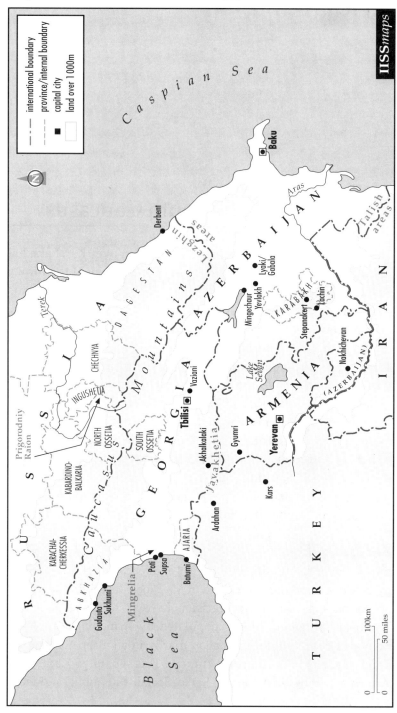

them dependent on Moscow for 'protection' against the Azerbaijani authorities if their 'autonomy' was infringed. At the same time, Azerbaijan relied on the Soviet leadership to ensure that the Armenians in Karabakh remained passive.[2] Despite ensuing tensions, occasional unrest and repeated Armenian demands for the boundaries to be redrawn, this formula remained in place until the advent of Gorbachev's *glasnost*.

By 1988, tensions between Armenians and Azeris throughout Karabakh had become open, and rapidly spread to Armenia and Azerbaijan, where nationalists began to challenge the pro-Moscow leadership in both republics. Following widespread disturbances and an armed takeover of Baku by Soviet troops in January 1990, a state of emergency was declared in the Karabakh capital, Stepanakert. In August, the Armenian Supreme Soviet announced its intention to declare independence and annex Karabakh. By the end of 1991, both countries had mobilised for full-scale war as Azerbaijan imposed an energy and transport blockade against Karabakh and the Armenian capital, Yerevan.

Although Azerbaijan scored some local successes in 1991–92, the Armenians captured Shusha, the main Azeri stronghold within Karabakh, in 1992. Agdam, a strategic district outside Karabakh's borders, fell in July 1993. Following the accession to power in Azerbaijan of Heydar Aliev in October 1993 and the reinforcement of the Azeri army, including some 1,500 mercenaries (among them several hundred Afghan *mujaheddin*), major offensives against Armenian forces took place in the southern Jebrail region in October and December. These failed, and on 12 May 1994 both parties signed a cease-fire, with a negotiated settlement intended to follow. Azerbaijan had lost almost all of Karabakh, together with several surrounding districts, accounting for about 14% of its territory. About 35,000 people were killed and more than a million made refugees, with approximately 700,000 Azeris from Karabakh and surrounding territories forced to move to other parts of the country, together with about 11,000 Kurds and 185,000 Azeris from Armenia. About 200,000 Armenians fled Azerbaijan.[3] Since then, the Armenian military has steadily improved its capacities, acquiring S-300 missiles and MiG-29 fighters from Russia and *Typhoon* missiles from China, making any Azerbaijani attempt to recapture lost territory by force extremely difficult.

Political Upheaval

Severe political instability in Azerbaijan, Armenia and Karabakh itself has accompanied the dispute. Between independence and Aliev's accession, five governments collapsed in Azerbaijan. Each was accused by opponents of being too close to Moscow, Ankara, Tehran or some combination of the three, and each was accused of 'selling out' Karabakh through weak negotiation or compromises with Yerevan. Armenian politics, although seemingly more stable in the early years of independence, began to fall apart by the end of 1997 as regional clans, mafia bosses and local warlords vied for power and influence. In February 1998, President Levon Ter-Petrossian was forced from power, and replaced by the more hawkish Robert Kocharian, the former leader of Karabakh and thus technically a citizen of Azerbaijan. On 27 October 1999, Prime Minister Vazgen Sarkissian and Chairman of the Parliament Karen Demirchian were shot dead during a session of parliament, prompting a six-month reshuffle of power to save Kocharian's regime.[4] In Karabakh itself, which declared independence in 1991, 'President' Arkadii Ghukasian was injured in an assassination attempt in March 2000.[5] Former army commander and defence minister Samvel Babaian was arrested along with his brother Karen, the mayor of Stepanakert and a former interior minister. The Babaians, leaders of one of Karabakh's most powerful clans, had been engaged in a power struggle with Ghukasian and his prime minister, Anushavan Danielian (a representative of a leading Armenian mafia group with links to Crimea).[6] Internal divisions in Karabakh are partly extensions of rivalries in Armenia itself, just as the Karabakh issue is used to feed intramural enmity in Baku. The strength of both the Armenian and Karabakh militaries, moreover, has meant a disproportionate and growing political role for the armed forces.[7]

Peace Efforts

This instability hindered attempts to reach a negotiated settlement to the dispute. Each time Armenia and Azerbaijan appeared close to compromise, elements in each country worked to replace the governments, or to stall negotiations. The first attempt to end the war took place under the auspices of Yeltsin and Kazak President

Nursultan Nazarbayev in September 1991. This failed when both sides launched major offensives within days of the peace communiqué. An attempt to restart talks two months later also failed when Armenian forces shot down the helicopter carrying Russian and Kazak observers to the negotiations. The next peace attempt was made in mid-1992, when Turkey offered to mediate following Armenian attacks on Nakhichevan, a strategic area of Azerbaijan along the Turkish and Iranian borders. This initiative was quickly stalled by Russia's disinterest, which also contributed to the failure of a similar Iranian effort.

In June 1992, European states under the auspices of the Conference on Security and Cooperation in Europe (CSCE, later the OSCE) assembled to discuss the worsening conflict.[8] What came to be called the 'Minsk Group' oversaw most negotiations between 1992 and 2001. By 1997, France, Russia and the US had assumed joint chairmanship, while Azerbaijan had agreed to participation in the talks by Armenian representatives from Karabakh.[9] The group devised a formula to reconcile the seemingly contradictory application of two central principles laid down by the 1975 Helsinki Final Act that established the CSCE: the Azerbaijani insistence on the sanctity of international borders; and the Armenian commitment to the right of self-determination. Mediators proceeded along four main lines of negotiation:

- Karabakh would be considered independent *de facto* but not *de jure*: that is, it would be granted the 'highest level of autonomy' from Baku, but would remain part of Azerbaijan;
- full withdrawal of Armenian forces from Azerbaijani territory outside Karabakh;[10]
- security guarantees from outside powers; and
- the return and resettlement of refugees.[11]

Mediation continued without achieving a settlement and, by the end of 1999, the Minsk process appeared to have outlived its usefulness. Yet the principal negotiators from each country remained individually active, and succeeded in placing the peace effort within an international context.[12] Aliev and Kocharian continued to meet during 2000, and by early 2001 rumours were circulating of a forthcoming deal. Both men had incentives to reach an agreement. For Aliev, advancing age and ill-health suggested the need to prepare his succession (preferably for his son, Ilkham), while the large numbers of refugees still awaiting resettlement and the troubled state of his country's economy made it difficult to postpone negotiations. For Kocharian, there was the pressing need to end his country's isolation and reduce its dependence on Russia and Iran.[13] But both also faced strong internal opposition, which blurred the distinction between parochial ambitions and national calls to arms. Since 1998, both governments have reacted by adopting tougher positions as each came to see the status quo as politically safer than making the concessions necessary to reach a settlement.[14] Compromise became viewed as both imperative and undesirable – and, most of all, temporary.

The prospect of renewed war in Karabakh fluctuated but the desire of other states, especially neighbours, to stay immune from its effects grew more acute as the dispute lingered on.[15] During the early 1990s, the need to prevent a fresh conflict over Karabakh was admittedly not great for Iran, Russia and Turkey, while the US saw its role as little more than that of a disinterested, honest broker. Each government considered the dispute more as an opportunity to attract allies than as a genuine threat, and showed appropriate restraint when involvement led to expressions of concern by another. Despite formal security guarantees and, in the case of Russia, the presence of troops in the region, no major power intervened decisively in the conflict, nor allowed it to escalate into a wider war. But for each of these powers, remaining apart from renewed war has become increasingly difficult, just as their interest in preventing a fresh conflict has grown.

Russia's sensitivity towards its southern borders has increased since 1994 after two costly wars in Chechnya and the growth of US ambitions. Moscow would find it difficult to stay idle during any new Azerbaijani offensive against its Armenian ally. The incentive of the US and Turkey to control any renewed conflict has increased with growing commercial investment in the region. In 1993, Iran sent troops four kilometres into Azerbaijan to create a 'buffer zone' against the anticipated movement of up to 200,000 refugees across the border. Tehran may be able to keep its distance from a new war in Karabakh, but if it involved Russia or Turkey, if it spread once again to Nakhichevan, or if it involved sizeable Azerbaijani conquests of what is now Armenian territory along the Iranian and Turkish borders, keeping aloof would require considerable restraint.

America's Inhibition

For the US, domestic politics and strong ties with regional states, namely Armenia and Turkey, hindered efforts to bring about a final settlement to the Karabakh dispute. The aims of local actors are of course more pertinent, but understanding the domestic limitations on outside powers helps to temper the accusation, often heard in the region, that the US simply lacks the will to get things done. Although it played no direct role in the war, the US did allow support to reach the Armenian side, and did not strongly discourage those who sought to help the Azeris. Although intimately involved in the many Karabakh negotiations since 1994, US officials appeared reluctant to take a tough negotiating stance towards either party, for fear of jeopardising the fragile US relationship with Aliev, or of provoking the powerful domestic Armenian lobby. For many years, this lobby has succeeded in forcing Congress to reject efforts to repeal the Section 907 restrictions on US assistance to Azerbaijan written into the 1992 Freedom Support Act. In mid-2000, it also forced on to the agenda legislation condemning Turkey for its massacre of Armenians in 1915 – a resolution which was only dropped under the most intense pressure from the White House, the State Department and the Pentagon. Although unrelated to Karabakh, the resolution caused outrage in Turkey and badly strained relations with Ankara. Domestic pressure from the Armenian lobby also coincided with increased US investment and interest in Azerbaijan during the mid-1990s, and a more contentious political atmosphere. Other interest groups came to realise that not only was peace in Karabakh a prerequisite for the development of the 'Eurasian energy corridor', but also that a new war there would call for greater attention from the US government, particularly if the Baku–Ceyhan oil pipeline went ahead. Although not intended to pass directly through Karabakh, the proposed route would run just 20km from its border, putting it at risk of sabotage in the event of fresh conflict.[16]

Russia's Ambivalence

The general Western view of Russia's role in the Karabakh dispute runs as follows: reluctant to accept an end to its hegemony, Russia continued to divide and rule the weaker nations to its south, in this case supporting the Karabakh Armenians against Azerbaijan throughout the 1990s. This effort was consistent with Russia's desire to maintain a decisive voice in Caucasian affairs, and with its historic sympathies with the Armenian struggle. At the same time, it gave succour to Azerbaijan in order to ensure some control over its prosecution of the war. When it appeared that Russia might lose this control, its forces conspired to replace pro-Turkish leader Elchibey with former KGB major-general and Politburo member Aliev. All this manoeuvring was designed to exclude Turkey and the US from Russia's traditional sphere of influence, particularly once large numbers of Western investors and diplomats began to arrive in Baku.

In truth, Russia has been more ambivalent about its interests in Karabakh, as more generally. Many Russians are nostalgic for the time when this and other territories were connected to their own, but as far as ordinary people (rather than government élites) are concerned, this reflects a nostalgia for the peace, security and living standards associated with that era, rather than any renewed imperial impulse. And even government élites have no desire to rule the southern Caucasus directly. Soon after becoming president, Putin repeated a common Russian paraphrase of Churchill's on socialism: 'Those who don't regret the dissolution of the USSR have no heart, and those who dream of its restoration in its previous form have no brains'.[17]

There does nonetheless appear to be a consensus that Russia should have some form of sphere of influence in former Soviet territories. There is little doubt that a US or NATO presence there irks many Russians. Russia furnished weapons to both sides during the Karabakh war, and continues to supply Armenia. Russian fears of Turkey persist, particularly now that Turkey's military is by most measures stronger than Russia's. But this does not mean that Russian leaders would start a war with Turkey on behalf of the Karabakh Armenians, or seek to make the entire Caucasus completely off-limits to the West. Russia's concern over some future

Turkish threat and a wish to initiate action against Azerbaijan are quite distinct; unless severely provoked, Moscow is unlikely to pursue the latter to assuage the former.

Russia still wishes to maintain leverage over both the Armenian and Azerbaijani governments, not because its leaders want to rule or annex the territory, but because they want to prevent military alliances with the West. But this does not preclude other, non-military Western influences, nor does it prevent Russia from establishing economic ties with apparently 'competing' states. Lukoil is a member of nearly all the Caspian consortia, and Russia is a key export route for both Azeri and Kazak oil. Russia has important economic links with Turkey, ranging from the Gazprom-backed 'Blue Stream' gas pipeline to an annual bilateral trade turnover of about $2bn. Turkish construction companies play a very important role in Russia, including in prestigious state projects. At the official level, therefore, both Russia and Turkey have sought to play down any innate or overall national rivalry. With regard to Armenia, Russia does not oppose the economic involvement of outsiders. So long as Armenia remains close to Russia strategically, a better environment for its economically wrecked ally is considered positive.

Russian involvement in the South Caucasus is also designed to project the appearance of being able to control the outer limits of Russia's 'strategic' borders, seen as coterminous with those of the former Soviet Union. Russian attempts to impose order are frequently portrayed in the West as coercion, but they can also involve courtship. Russia has, for example, undertaken to withdraw from two of its four bases in Georgia with, presumably, the partial understanding that the Georgian government would clamp down on Chechen rebel activity on its territory. While Moscow could conceivably use any Georgian failure to do so as a pretext for direct interference, this dual aspect of a larger power's influence over a smaller neighbour is by no means unique to Russian policy.

The South Caucasus will also remain prominent in Russia's overall strategic calculus because of its status as one of the two key flank zones in the Conventional Forces in Europe (CFE) Treaty. The status of the treaty is unclear given Russia's violations in Chechnya and Armenia, and in 1997 Moscow negotiated a new interpretation of the flank limit allowing it considerably more troops, causing consternation in Baku and pleas for reassurance from US officials.[18] Russia is also obliged to defend Armenia under the terms of the 1992 Tashkent Collective Security Treaty and the 1997 bilateral Treaty of Friendship, Cooperation and Mutual Assistance. It maintains about 3,000 troops in the country, as well as a large base at Gyumri. Following its partial withdrawal from the Georgian base of Akhalkalaki in October 2000, Russia transferred 76 tanks to Gyumri, bringing the total to about 300. The previous month, Russia and Armenia signed a new Friendship Treaty that pledged further Russian support in seeking a solution to Karabakh.[19] Despite Armenia's efforts to diversify its international relationships, Russia has shown little interest in withdrawing from either commitment, and given deep-rooted Armenian fears of Turkey, it is doubtful that most Armenians would favour withdrawal. Russia will seek to preserve its influence in the South Caucasus in ways that do not incur large burdens. There is considerable distance between proof of truly imperial Russian ambitions in the South Caucasus, and the Russian activity that has so far taken place, which has been limited.

Turkey's Frustration

Turkey shares a border with all three South Caucasus states, and those areas considered by Ankara to be among the country's most vulnerable, namely Kurdish regions, are immediately to the south-east. During the Karabakh conflict, Turkey sealed its frontier with Armenia, provided substantial assistance to the Azerbaijani side, and came close to intervening directly in 1992 following an Armenian attack on Nakhichevan. The consensus now in Ankara is in favour of a more restrained and detached stance towards the Caucasus and, so long as Turkey views the repeated demands for greater attention from parties in both Armenia and Azerbaijan as nuisances rather than serious priorities, its policy will continue to stagnate. This could change if either Russia or Iran pursue more aggressive policies, but neither is likely to do so initially.

If a new war between Armenia and Azerbaijan over Karabakh spread to Nakhichevan, as it briefly did again in 1993, this would provide Turkey with a more palpable pretext to intervene, though the most compelling pressure to do so would come from domestic political sources, rather than from any serious threat to the border. Turkey's politics are complex and fluctuating, but marked generally by a three-way struggle between a pro-Western tradition, most powerfully represented in the military and the state bureaucracy; a pro-Russia lobby, particularly comprising industrialists; and a Turanist, or pan-Turkic, tendency among intellectuals and politicians keen on extending Turkish influence over the country's eastern and southern neighbours. A fourth, more conservative and neo-Ottoman tradition has been linked with the latter group, as have religious activists who seek a greater role for Turkey in the Islamic world. Because of its support in the military and among the Turkish élite, the first group is usually seen to prevail over the others.

These conflicting positions have informed Turkey's role in the South Caucasus insofar as they have fed individual ambitions and agendas. In 1995, for example, rogue Turkish intelligence operatives were alleged to have designed Azeri opposition leader Mahir Javadov's coup attempt against Aliev, although Javadov was commonly linked to groups in Iran and Russia. Rivalry between one-time Turkish presidents Turgut Özal and Suleyman Demirel resulted in each trying to outdo the other in cultivating relationships with the newly-independent Turkic states. Özal even argued in favour of direct intervention in the Karabakh war. His death from a heart attack following a visit to Baku in April 1993 marked the end of Turkish support for Elchibey, the increasingly ineffective and unpopular Azerbaijani leader. Aliev was present at Özal's funeral as a visiting 'head of state' (citing his authority in his Nakhichevan homeland), and shortly afterwards assumed power in Baku. There were suspicions that Turkey, rather than Russia, was behind Aliev's return to power, for reasons ranging from simple lack of confidence in Elchibey to the highly fanciful theory that, during his KGB days in the 1960s, Aliev recruited Demirel, and the two had plotted together ever since. But there remains considerable suspicion of Aliev in Turkish circles, given the allegedly central role he played in directing covert Soviet support to Kurdish militant groups during the same period.[20]

Demirel in turn invested significant time in nurturing ties with both Aliev and Georgian leader Shevardnadze. He also led the effort to convince Azerbaijan, Georgia and the US to support the

Baku–Ceyhan export route. A Caucasus Stability Pact, resurrected by Demirel on the model of NATO's Balkans Stability Pact, became popular with local leaders, including in Armenia, as a way of diversifying their regional relationships.[21] The pact, which proposed regular consultations and a regional development plan, was seen as an attractive alternative to calls for NATO membership or bases, heard frequently in Azerbaijan and Georgia in 1998 and 1999, and was supported in principle by Iran and Russia.

The end of Demirel's presidency in 2000 did not put a stop to Turkey's attempts to win over the newly-independent South Caucasian states. His successor, Ahmet Necdet Sezer, selected Baku for his first foreign trip in August. Turkey's most pressing interest in a Karabakh peace has remained opening its border with Armenia, to allow for more convenient access to Azerbaijan and Central Asia, as well as securing supplies to meet its vast energy demands, notably for natural gas. Regional trade promotion has had an important impact on public opinion, particularly in response to local initiatives like the growing cooperation between the mayors of Gyumri and Kars.[22]

Turkey is not overly concerned by Armenian hostility, but it fears and resents the influence of the Armenian diaspora in the West. It also seeks to prevent its differences with Yerevan from complicating any issues associated with the Kurdish question, such as the Armenian takeover of the Lachin corridor, once populated predominantly by Kurds.[23] Although many Kurds have assimilated Azeri culture, a minority of Armenians still wish to mobilise whatever anti-Turkish sentiment exists among Kurds in or from Karabakh. Nonetheless, Turkish–Armenian relations improved in 2000, assisted by Demirel's Stability Pact proposal and Shevardnadze's quiet mediation with Azeri, Armenian and Turkish leaders. Turkey's focus became less the Armenian 'threat' *per se*, and more the wider balance of power that would emerge from a final solution to the Karabakh question.[24] Indeed, the standard Turkish view of Armenia does not mirror the Russian one of a 'tripwire' state: many forward-looking Turks, like some Westernised Armenians, do not believe that Armenia's status as a Russian proxy is destined to be permanent. Some may still be concerned about Russia, perhaps reflecting long-standing Russian fears dating back to the nineteenth-century obsession with the Bosphorus and the Dardanelles. However, these residual prejudices may recede with the passage of time, and Russia may no longer be seen as Turkey's main rival in the Caucasus. The alternative, of course, is Iran.

Despite the flow of gas from Turkmenistan to Turkey via Iran and a bilateral gas deal, competition between Iran and Turkey over Caspian oil pipelines will intensify. Until now, much of the Caspian pipeline discussion in the West has misconstrued Russia's role; much of the oil continues to pass through Russia, and Russian concerns participate in most consortia. Russia's own oil and gas sector competes only marginally for markets with those in the Caspian. The real question is whether Iran or Turkey will serve as the primary transit state for Caspian oil travelling to the West.[25]

In energy exports, and to a lesser extent even geopolitically, both Turkey and Iran have competed as much with Russia in the Caucasus as they have with one another. Although Russia and Iran enjoy good overall relations because of their compatible interests throughout Central Eurasia and in other areas, an improvement in Iran's relations with the US and the Arab world could lead to a strategic realignment. This may or may not affect Iran's relationship with Russia, but it most certainly would raise serious questions for Turkey, the West's principal non-Arab interlocutor (besides Israel) in the Middle East and the Mediterranean. This reordering of alliances could be further complicated by the growing activity of Sunni radical groups in Turkey itself, leading to even more insecure and volatile Turkish governments. Domestic pressure to intervene on behalf of neighbouring 'Turks' in the Caucasus could grow, along with the need on the part of future Turkish governments to offset the fear of both regional and global isolation in the event that Turkey is faced with a remote, but not inconceivable, worst-case scenario: permanent marginalisation from Europe, and exclusive American backing for Egypt, Iran and Israel in the Middle East.

In the meantime, Turkey has shown little public concern over its longer-term position *vis-à-vis* Iran, and the ideological threat from a fragile Shi'i theocracy in Tehran is no longer taken very seriously. Of the principal threats to Turkish security, Iran ranks far below the Kurdish insurrection, Iraq, Greece or even Syria.[26] Turkey would intentionally enter into conflict in the Caucasus only if it believed that it risked a major and humiliating loss of influence relative to Russia or Iran, and if – as a result of a new Armenian–Azeri war – domestic opinion in Turkey clamoured for intervention on behalf of neighbouring 'Turks'.[27] The country that would gain most from a major conflict between Turkey and Russia, over Karabakh or some other issue, would be Iran, because its economic and political position would almost certainly improve at the expense both of Moscow and Ankara.

Iran's Prudence

Even without renewed conflict in Karabakh, geography suggests an important role for Iran in the South Caucasus. Yet, whether through caution, humility, distraction or ignorance, Tehran has been reluctant to become deeply involved. Iran's main interests are more modest: securing a peaceful and open northern border; ending the country's international isolation; and expanding its links to the Black Sea and Europe.

Iran also has to contend with the sensitivities of the approximately 20m ethnic Azeris who live in the north (over twice the population of Azerbaijan itself). As yet, this group has posed no organised threat to the state, and few Iranian Azeris have demonstrated any real passion for irredentism; pan-Azeri nationalism has been more common in Azerbaijan, but has been largely quiet since the ousting of Elchibey. Despite the Iranian government's support for Armenia during the war, it knows that it must maintain cordial, if not warm, relations with Azerbaijan if it wishes to keep irredentism from ever taking hold.

Aside from its incursion into Azerbaijan and supplying Armenia with oil, Iran played a largely passive role in the Karabakh conflict. It attempted to mediate in 1992, although by May, Armenian forces had captured the strategic town of Shusha, while Baku had succumbed to political chaos amid the ousting of pro-Moscow President Ayaz Mutalibov. Neither side was able or willing to compromise, public opinion in Iran had grown hostile to Armenia, and the setbacks suffered by their fellow Shi'a in Azerbaijan mattered less to Iranians than the affront to their sponsored cease-fire and the more pressing threat the Armenian advance posed to the Lachin corridor, and hence to Nakhichevan.[28] The potential for unrest among Azeris on both sides of the Iranian border would significantly increase in the event of Armenia seizing Nakhichevan. Thus, territorial priorities relating to its northern border were more pressing for the Iranian government than any broader cultural or political rivalry.

Fluctuating politics in both Azerbaijan and Armenia could still draw Iran more deeply into affairs in the Caucasus. Kocharian has tried to preserve Armenia's tactical alliance with Iran against Turkey, and to bolster his alliance with Russia. The Iranian government has been careful to avoid being trapped by any contradictions that emerge between Armenia's anti-Turkish and pro-Russian positions. In Azerbaijan, the Musavat party, which led the country during its brief independence in 1918–20, has become markedly friendlier towards Iran since the mid-1990s, despite its pan-Turkic character. Musavat leader Isa Gambar's reasons are complex, and have to do with disenchantment with Turkish support for his enemies in the government. He also resents the inadequate backing Turkey gave to previous regimes, mainly the nominally pro-Turkish Elchibey's, as well as to his own when he was in power in 1992.[29] Finally, there are suspicions that Aliev's numerous personal connections to both Iran and Turkey are serving the interests of his inner circle at the expense of the country. Yet any new overtures to Iran would be made amid strong anti-Iranian feeling in Azerbaijan as a whole.[30]

Following the failure of its mediation effort in 1992, Iran offered itself as an alternative to the Minsk Group, and occasionally raised Karabakh in wider fora like the Organisation of the Islamic Conference (OIC). Yet these gestures have been muted by Iran's desire for good relations with Russia and the Arab states, which have been unmoved by events involving their fellow Muslims in the Caucasus. Ties to the Middle East have expanded, but not for reasons associated with Islam. Armenia's relations with Lebanon and Syria have deepened through the Armenian diaspora in those countries. Azerbaijan, especially under Elchibey, has engaged heavily with Israel. Israelis have made sizeable investments in the country, and were rumoured in 1997 and 1998 to be collaborating with the US in constructing major listening posts against Iran on Azerbaijani territory.[31] To the extent that any of these connections matter, they serve merely to broaden the pool of interests Iran has in the South Caucasus.

Ultimately, relations with Russia and Turkey matter most to Iran's government, however divided it may be in general. Many Iranians have long presumed that their country's geographic advantage gives them the upper hand. During a 1992 visit, journalist Thomas Goltz recorded an Iranian official as saying:

> *Iran was not playing the same game as Turkey. If there was any race, it should be compared to the story of the tortoise and the hare. The Turks were investing all sorts of money in television, the press, and high profile visits in an effort to dominate the new republics. But this was a short-term policy that would explode in their faces when the local cultures decided to define their own place in the sun. The Turks were likely to lose a lot of money – and respect – when that happened. Iran's policy, in contrast, was one based on regional stability and allowing the new republics to make up their own minds about where their interests and identities lay.*[32]

A struggle between Turkey and Iran for the hearts and minds of Central Eurasia has never taken place to the extent predicted in the West, because it was cast improperly in ideological or theological terms. More likely is a contest between Iran and Turkey that is narrowly strategic, involving the regional prestige leaders of each state seek to amass against their rivals at home and abroad. In a sign of this emerging pattern, the US government's announcement in March 2000 of a relaxation of sanctions on Iranian luxury goods necessitated repeated assurances to Ankara that this 'Washington–Tehran *rapprochement*' would not weaken ties with Turkey.[33] The attempted normalisation with Iran was limited even under the Clinton administration, and the new Bush administration has expressed similar caution, with tough statements attacking Iran for 'supporting international terrorism', and criticising Russia for supplying arms to Tehran. In consequence, the chances of a substantial Iranian route for Caspian oil have considerably diminished, at least in the short to medium term, and the Russia–

Iran axis against the influence of the US and Turkey will remain a factor in the region. Nonetheless, the assurances given to Turkey by the Clinton administration illustrate just how allergically Ankara reacts to any signs of a closer US–Iranian relationship. They also respond to the serious implications any competition between Turkey and Iran are presumed to have for a country like Azerbaijan, whose people perceive themselves to be spread across Iranian and Turkish spheres of influence. The mere existence of an independent Azeri state can still be considered a threat to Iranian patriotism, while it serves as a distant temptation for Turkish nationalists.[34] This feeling of divided heritage is shared by many Central Asians. It also corresponds to the view in each of the region's small states that local rivalries are outgrowths to one degree or another of competition between the US and their larger neighbours, despite the marginal role they have played in what have been internal conflicts.

Outcome

Persistent popular discontent with corruption and economic stagnation has caused serious difficulties for the governments of both Armenia and Azerbaijan. This has made a tough stance on Karabakh even more important, but harder to sustain, both for Aliev and for Kocharian.[35] Under these conditions, the ambiguity and ambivalence of the policies of external actors have frustrated the ambitions of local allies. More precarious conditions on the ground could easily inflame the latent antagonism that still predominates throughout the Caucasus. The breakdown of a peace settlement and a new war in Karabakh may be averted by Kocharian and Aliev, or by their successors. But if it is not, the damage it could do to relations between Russia and Turkey and Turkey and Iran is likely to be greater than it was during the last war. The US role would also be both more important, and more difficult to clarify because of the large increase in Western investment in Azerbaijan during the mid-1990s, and the undiminished power of the Armenian lobby in the US. The ambiguity of security commitments on the part of all the relevant actors, along with mixed messages about the relationship between energy schemes and strategic affairs, suggests that rivalry has ceased to be a masquerade for the governments of Iran, Turkey, Russia and the US. The question now is how the incubation of rivalry in the South Caucasus compares with the strategic interests of these powers, along with those of China, India and Pakistan, to the east of the Caspian.

Chapter 3

Ferghana and Central Asia

The major powers have tended to see Central Asia more as a volatile font of transnational threats than, like the South Caucasus, an area in which to seek leverage over one another. This distinction has, however, become less marked in recent years. An important question is whether this increased outside interest has worsened regional instabilities, or whether the regional situation would have deteriorated even if left alone.

China, Iran, Russia and the US have all tended to react to the perceived threats emanating from the region, notably Islamic networks and narcotics, in ways that have furthered the imbalance of power among the regional states. In turn, this has led to a greater and more precarious dependence on external support. The reactions of the Kyrgyz, Tajik and Uzbek governments to events in and around Ferghana demonstrate how these regimes have manipulated the vulnerabilities they so frequently condemned as threats to regional order. To attract external support for their unpopular regimes, they portrayed largely internal problems – notably Islamic radicalism – as having both external origins, and external answers.

Background

About 170km wide and 300km long, the Ferghana valley connects Kyrgyzstan, Tajikistan and Uzbekistan. It is surrounded on three sides by high mountains that divide each nation's section of the valley from most of its home territory. Within the valley itself,

Map 3 Ferghana and Central Asia

however, there are no natural barriers. It was a single political unit under the Khanate of Quqand until the boundaries of the Soviet republics were drawn up in the 1920s, and even thereafter frontiers were difficult to detect on the ground.

Steep population growth, the rapid urbanisation of people from traditional rural cultures, inadequate employment and severe ecological degradation throughout the region all suggest a familiar recipe for social collapse. Ferghana is the most densely populated area of Central Asia; there are approximately ten million people in the valley, or about 250 per square kilometre. In places, densities run as high as 2,300. Nearly 75% are Uzbek, about 20% Kyrgyz and the remainder Tajik.[1] The valley is important to each country: nearly half of Kyrgyzstan's population lives there, and half of its industrial and agricultural output comes from its two valley *oblasts*, Osh and Jalalabad; most of Uzbekistan's sources of oil and water originate in the valley, as does about 25% of its cotton supply; 75% of Tajikistan's arable land and 65% of its industrial production come from one valley *oblast*, Leninabad (also known by its capital city, Khujand).

Stability in Ferghana has been a central concern for regional governments, as well as a focal point for groups that oppose them. Yet the region's post-Soviet, autocratic, clan-based regimes have done little to remedy the underlying causes of instability. Nearly all post-Soviet conflicts in Central Asia have taken place in Ferghana; the one exception, the Tajik civil war, has had close links to it. Ferghana has also played a central role in the worsening of relations between regional states, and between them and larger countries like China, Russia and the US.

Episodes of Conflict

The first conflict involving the Ferghana valley took place in 1989, when a market dispute between 'Meskhetian Turks' (a people deported from Georgia to Central Asia by Stalin) and Uzbeks in the city of Ferghana in Uzbekistan's portion of the valley escalated into armed clashes.[2] In June 1990, long-standing tensions between Uzbeks and Kyrygz in the cities of Osh and Uzgen escalated into riots which left some 200 people dead. Although there has been no repeat, ethnic tensions in these cities remain high, and poor relations between the Uzbek and Kyrgyz governments have only made matters worse. Tensions also increased between Kyrgyz and Tajik communities in other areas. It is important to note that inter-ethnic conflict has been between Central Asians. Mass ethnic violence has not yet been directed to any great extent against Slavs. Official Russian policy claiming to support the welfare of ethnic Russians abroad has in fact done little for them, but this restraint may be put to a more difficult test in the event of any significant organised repression of Russians, or large-scale physical attacks on them.

Ferghana has also seen official persecution of religious and political activists, above all in Uzbekistan. Tension between the Uzbek authorities and Islamists began in the city of Namangan in late 1991 with the rise of the *Adolat* (Justice) movement. *Adolat* took control of the regional government, and imposed a mild form of Islamic rule. When it went from improving community services in Namangan to attacking the official clergy and the legitimacy of Karimov's regime, the government's tolerance reached an end. Since then, Karimov has made it his mission to 'smash' any sign of political Islam in his country. By early 1992, he had replaced the regional governor and begun to persecute the movement's leaders. Many fled to neighbouring countries; others went underground and established contacts with other Islamic groups.

In late 1997, another round of violence broke out in Namangan following the beheading of a senior police official. Karimov initiated another major crackdown, accusing his enemies in Ferghana of being part of the network supporting insurgents in Chechnya, Afghanistan and Pakistan. Nearly 1,000 suspected militants were arrested in Namangan and Andijon, curfews were imposed and the use of loudspeakers at mosques was forbidden.[3] Both *Adolat* and the Uzbek branch of the Islamic Renaissance Party (IRP), a movement of Islamists active to varying degrees throughout the former Soviet Union and outlawed for nearly a decade, now experienced direct persecution of a far more serious nature. Perhaps most worrying for the Karimov regime has been the *Hizb-ut Tahrir*, or Liberation Party, which was formed in February 1998 by former members of *Adolat*. Unlike more expressly militant groups, *Hizb-ut Tahrir* has prioritised political mobilisation through strong local ties, particularly with teachers and other members of the lower-middle class.

The Uzbek government has loosely termed all these move-ments '*Wahhabi*'. The name derives from a Saudi-based theological movement, but has been used throughout the Soviet Union since the early 1980s to refer to any variety of radical Islam. As with the Russian government's response to similar uprisings in Chechnya and Dagestan, Karimov's use of the *Wahhabi* label made these groups synonymous with terrorism, barbarism and conflict. Ferghana, with its tradition of religious activism and proximity to much of the human and ideological spill-over from conflicts in Tajikistan and Afghanistan, was rapidly identified as the chief regional hotspot.[4]

The fourth principal conflict in Ferghana followed Uzbekis-tan's intervention in the 1992–97 civil war in Tajikistan on behalf of displaced ethnic Uzbek factions from Khujand. Its origins lay in the main outcome of the Tajik conflict: a power-sharing agreement between the government, led by Kulobis under President Emomali Rakhmanov, and the United Tajik Opposition (UTO), an umbrella organisation that included representatives of the Islamic parties (principally the Tajik IRP) and groups mainly from the Gharm valley. The other main regional bloc, the Pamiris (Isma'ili Muslims from Gorno-Badakhshan), was given significant autonomy. Left out of the settlement were the Khujand Uzbeks, who had dominated Tajikistan for most of the Soviet period, and subsequently under Abdulmalik Abdullojanov, prime minister in 1992–93.[5]

The exclusion of the Khujandis from the peace settlement led to the withdrawal of official Uzbek support for the agreement, as well as strong criticism by Tashkent of the inclusion of members of the IRP, who were said to be Islamists working on behalf of foreign sponsors. This provided the pretext for the invasion of Khujand by the ethnic Laqai (or assimilated Uzbek) Colonel Makhmud Khudoiberdyev in November 1998. Khudoiberdyev had held a key post in the Soviet army in Qurghonteppa, and went on to amass a large militia after independence. His usefulness to the new Tajik government allowed him to take control of the country's largest aluminium plant, and several other lucrative businesses.[6] By early 1996, he had fallen out with the Kulobi-dominated government, and fled to Uzbekistan after a failed attempt to capture Dushanbe. The Khujand incursion, which was widely assumed to have been sponsored by Abdullojanov and the Uzbek government, was defeated, and Khudoiberdyev went into hiding in Uzbekistan.

Former UTO fighters, notably Uzbek militants of the Islamic Movement of Uzbekistan (IMU) under Juma Namangoni, also turned to violence in the wake of the civil war. Namangoni appears to have made common cause with some former members of *Adolat* in 1998, and both groups were rumoured to include former members of the Uzbek IRP. Karimov blamed the IMU for bomb attacks in Tashkent in February 1999 which left scores of people dead, and which Karimov himself barely survived.[7] In August, about 1,000 militants claiming allegiance to Namangoni emerged from Tajikistan, crossed into Kyrgyzstan and seized several villages in the Batken and Chon-Alai *raions*. They also took several hundred people hostage, including the Kyrgyz interior ministry commander Anarbek

Shamkeev and four Japanese geologists. The militants demanded the release of 5,000 prisoners from Uzbek jails (many of whom were put there after the Tashkent bombings) and announced their intent to launch a holy war against the Uzbek government from Sokh, its largely Tajik-populated enclave in the Kyrgyz portion of the Ferghana valley. The incident ended in October, after the Japanese government supplied Kyrgyzstan with the funds to pay a reported $50,000 ransom. Most of the militants crossed back into Tajikistan, before moving on to Afghanistan, where they established a base near Kunduz. A new round of insurgency gripped the region in August 2000, with attacks reported in Surkhandaria in southern Uzbekistan, in the Izboskan district of Andijon near the Kyrygz border and in Bostanlyk, about 80km from Tashkent.

Incidents like that at Batken are important more because of the state rivalries they bring to the surface than from any immediate threat of full-scale war. During the hostage crisis, Karimov was extremely critical of both the Tajik and Kyrgyz governments: the latter for not dealing more resolutely with the insurgency, and the former for allowing it to happen in the first place.[8] Both governments responded that too strong a reaction would play into the hands of the militants and put the hostages at risk. In August, Uzbekistan's air force bombed Kyrgyz and Tajik territory. Following the Batken crisis, the Tajik government cracked down on Islamic radicals, and Kyrgyzstan increased its defence spending by almost 50%.[9] New border posts were established, and a new *oblast*, appropriately called Batken, was created in order to make it easier to contain future incidents. Although a joint command centre was established in Khujand, and the Tajik, Uzbek and Kyrgyz governments all announced a common policy of 'annihilation', both Kyrgyzstan and Uzbekistan accused Tajikistan of helping the militants.[10] The Uzbek government repeatedly claimed to have the situation under control, but Karimov himself criticised his military's inadequate response.

A Regional Cauldron

Unrest in and around Ferghana is significant because it is taking place within a wider disequilibrium among the regional states. According to Uzbekistan, the latest conflict, like the earlier incidents in Namangan, was the work of hostile external forces intent on imposing a new caliphate in Central Asia. These forces are apparently associated with similar *Wahhabi* movements in Afghanistan, Pakistan and Chechnya, and so demand a co-ordinated response from all the region's secular regimes.[11] The problem with this conspiracy theory is that it is not fully shared by all governments, despite their public displays of solidarity. They may be frustrated with the failure to defend their borders adequately, but they are even more concerned over the pretext such incidents offer Uzbekistan or Russia to dictate policies that run counter to the preferences of weaker states. Since the 1999 and 2000 crises, the Uzbek government has significantly improved its defence capacities and strengthened its border controls, in some cases unilaterally demarcating the frontier several kilometres inside neighbouring countries. Local inhabitants, for example in southern Kazakstan, have been outraged.[12] Not only have their villages been split between two territories, but they have also been made to suffer the imposition of a new and unfamiliar set of controls for no apparent reason other than to proclaim which distant authority happens to be in charge.

The ramifications of these actions are better understood when considered in light of the weakness of state institutions throughout the region. Both Kyrgyzstan and Tajikistan are very difficult to govern. Each is divided by mountains that are impassable for much of the year; each is prone to severe sectional rivalries; and each is isolated from the outside world. Each also has to contend with significant populations of Tajiks and Kyrgyz outside their home territory, as well as large concentrations of Uzbeks within. Indeed, Uzbekistan is the only state with large ethnic populations in every neighbouring state, as well as a large majority within its borders. Its size and power have produced a geopolitical imbalance so severe that headlines such as 'Kyrgyzstan: here today, gone tomorrow' and 'Tajikistan: a tail with no head' are commonly used in the local press.[13] Both countries feel cheated by Soviet-era borders that favour Uzbekistan; Tajikistan in particular feels the loss of its historic cultural centres, Bukhara and Samarkand. Strong inferiority complexes have led each state to try to reduce Uzbek control over their export routes and energy supplies.[14] The fear they have for their survival has as much to do with Uzbekistan as it does with their multiple internal problems. Kyrgyz alarmists proclaim that their country eventually will have no choice but to become a protectorate or province of Kazakstan because of Uzbek coercion. Their Tajik counterparts believe it is only a matter of time before Tashkent reconstitutes the old Khanate of Bukhara and annexes Khujand, as well as the rest of Tajikistan except Gorno-Badakhshan, which in turn might merge with the Badakhshan portion of Afghanistan.[15]

The relevance of Ferghana to regional security therefore comes from its association with wider concerns, like the spread of Islamic militancy, the transnational proliferation of the narcotics trade, the underlying fragility of the regional states and their worsening relations with one another. Competition over the regional narcotics trade in particular became fierce towards the middle of the 1990s. In 1998, drugs traffic through the Ferghana valley was estimated to have increased three-fold over the previous year.[16] Control over such trade has become critical for both local governments and outside players, namely Russia, Uzbekistan and warring factions in Afghanistan. These and similar threats, which appeared initially to be isolated within states, have tended to become inter-state problems that threaten regional peace.

The quest for alliances with external powers has become an obsession for every regional government. Both Kazakstan and Kyrgyzstan appointed foreign ministers fluent in Mandarin, and quickly set about planning visits for their leaders to Beijing. Tajikistan's government has relied on Russian sponsorship of its peace accord, and has hinted that its previously loose ties with Iran might be strengthened.[17] And every government has to varying degrees sought to attract greater Western support. The response of the outside world has, however, been mixed.

Western Indifference

The US and most of the West have remained largely indifferent – despite much rhetoric to the contrary. Throughout the 1990s, regional governments entertained hopes of military assistance, but were convinced by the end of the decade that any such assistance, except Russian, would only be symbolic. The US, the UK, France, Turkey and China all provided assistance packages to the three Ferghana states, as well as to Kazakstan in the wake of the 1999

Batken incidents, but none exceeded $10m. Most involved modest transfers of military hardware and training programmes. The US government sent the directors of the Federal Bureau of Investigation and the Central Intelligence Agency (CIA), as well as Secretary of State Madeleine Albright, to the region in March and April 2000, and added the IMU to its list of foreign terrorist organisations the following September. But other US policy aims, namely promoting human rights and economic reform, caused problems during Albright's visit, and it has proved difficult to convince a sceptical American public that these states deserve serious help.

American attempts to make 'strategic pillars' of any of the Central Asian states were bound to fail in any case because doing so was incompatible with overall post-Cold War US foreign policy, and because it was impossible to pick and choose among imperfect regional allies in the absence of a clear strategic imperative. Even with such an imperative, as during the Cold War, US leaders were ambivalent about their relationships with figures like Ngo Dinh Diem, Anastasio Somoza, the Shah of Iran and Gamal Abdel Nasser, who once advised an American friend: 'if you want the cooperation of any Middle Eastern leader you must first understand his limitations – the limitations placed on him by the emotions and the suspicions of the people he leads – and be reconciled to the fact that you can never ask him to go beyond those limitations. If you feel you *must* have him go beyond them, you must be prepared to help him lessen the limitations'.[18] In post-Cold War Central Eurasia, lessening the limitations was seen to carry too high a price given the lack of vital US interests in the region. Yet even the limited US engagement that has occurred has been enough to worry other major powers. Although all the outside players have a common interest in combating Sunni Islamist radicalism, their mutual rivalry has actually made the achievement of this goal much more difficult.

China's Fear

China's north-western province of Xinjiang borders Kazakstan, Kyrgyzstan and Tajikistan, and lies just over the Tien Shan range from Ferghana. Stabilising China's north-western borders has been a priority for Beijing: since 1992, agreements have been signed with all three states which resolve all demarcation questions, except for a few with Tajikistan over remote sections of the Pamirs. China's reasons for paying considerable attention to events in Ferghana are two-fold: to weaken both the cause of ethnic separatism in Xinjiang and external support for it; and better to integrate the province economically with the rest of China, and with the Central Asian states across the border. Beijing sees improving the economic well-being of Xinjiang as necessary in order to reconcile the local inhabitants to its rule, as well as to support China's regional presence. Most of the 15 border crossings from Xinjiang are open, and the Chinese government claims to be committed to improving infrastructure to the tune of an estimated $8.45bn over the next five years.[19] For these reasons, China has been eager to cooperate with the regional states in ways that appear disproportionate to their size and influence.

Yet China's paranoia over ethnic separatism in Xinjiang is difficult to exaggerate. This is ironic given that most of the rhetoric in support of independence for the Uighurs, a Muslim Turkic population of about eight million, has come from compatriots in Turkey and the US. Xinjiang also has about two million Kazaks near the Ili valley, and smaller numbers of Kyrgyz, Tajiks, Mongols and Hui (Chinese Muslims).[20] Although none of these groups has organ-ised a serious threat to Chinese authority, this has not prevented Beijing from repressing even the slightest signs of irredentism. China's fear of 'splittists' joins a presumption about political Islam similar to that of Russians about the Northern Caucasus, and many Central Asians about Ferghana. For the Chinese authorities, Uighur unrest and Islamic terrorism are one and the same, particularly because Uighurs served in the Afghan war and were exposed to many of the same ideological influences as their Uzbek, Kyrgyz and Tajik counterparts. When Uighur activists based in Turkey claimed responsibility for blowing up a bus in Beijing in March 1997, the Chinese government declared that the explosives had come from Pakistan by way of Afghanistan. Subsequently, the Chinese Ministry of State Security warned that efforts by Islamic militants to 'infiltrate' China from the Middle East would pose an increasing threat.[21] Despite its willingness to expand trade links, these concerns led the Chinese government to suspend improvements to the Khunjerab pass and the Karakorum highway, and to place restrictions on border crossings to and from Pakistan. In addition to the activities of 'itinerant religious instructors', Chinese authorities have become more concerned about drug-smuggling and the lucrative trade in falcon chicks, which make their way through Pakistan to wealthy customers in the Gulf.[22]

With Ferghana increasingly viewed as the regional target of the *Wahhabis,* the Chinese government has intensified its collaboration with the Central Asian states in their efforts to repress 'religious extremists', whether Uighur, Uzbek or Tajik.[23] One expression of this trend is the 'Shanghai Five' mechanism, which was established in 1996 to resolve outstanding border disputes, reach agreement on mutual reductions in border troops and exchange information about deployments and exercises. It comprises China, Russia, Kazakstan, Kyrgyzstan and Tajikistan. In 1999, the group expanded into areas of law enforcement as regular meetings of the five interior ministers and intelligence chiefs were added to those of the defence and foreign ministers. This coincided with an increase in trade and bilateral agreements between China and the other states, as well as with Uzbekistan, which does not share a border with China but is still considered a 'neighbour'.[24] In 2000, the Shanghai Five summit for the first time included Uzbekistan's Karimov as an observer. Karimov had become increasingly vocal about the need to broaden ties with China, and in September 2000 took great pride in the opening of a tunnel through the Kamchik and Rezak passes, which facilitates Uzbekistan's connections to the Ferghana valley, and potentially to Xinjiang.[25]

The willingness of the Central Asian governments to co-operate with China has helped alleviate some of Beijing's concerns about separatist threats in Xinjiang. However, a number of factors could undermine the mood of cooperation. The first is anti-Chinese feeling in Central Asia. The roots of Sinophobia are largely cultural, and extend back through centuries of complex dealings between Chinese and Central Asian dynasties. Generations of Soviet propaganda indoctrinated anti-Chinese feeling, and Central Asians can still be heard talking of the 'threat' posed by thousands of Chinese people and products crossing the border. As a result, China has been careful to downplay its regional profile.

Secondly, China's leaders still give priority to Russia in the light of their conviction that it will recover its position as a great power. Central Asia is seen as one of the riskiest areas in which to challenge even a weakened Russia, compelling caution in Beijing.[26] China's growing demand for oil and gas from Kazakstan and Turkmenistan, and its need for water from the Kyrgyz side of the Tien Shan, all require a stable environment without serious rivalries.

The third factor is the apparent competition between Kazakstan, Kyrgyzstan and Uzbekistan for Chinese favour. Akaev, Karimov and Nazarbayev have all made high-profile visits to Beijing since 1994, and have boasted about their new special relationships with China's reforming leadership. Each went with a specific purpose: Akaev was keen to secure China's sponsorship of a new rail link over the Torugart pass rather than to Osh in the south, thus avoiding the Uzbek rail system; Karimov sought to promote his image as a world leader and to secure China's support for his anti-terrorism campaign; and Nazarbayev went to convince a reluctant Chinese government to subsidise the completion of an oil pipeline from Kazakstan on terms favourable to Kazak industry and workers.[27] As each appeared to upstage the other, China's government has grown more wary, and hesitant about future commitments.

Given the public nature of these overtures, the three governments would be in a difficult position if any future outbreak of unrest in Xinjiang led to Chinese cross-border attacks on Uighur sanctuaries. Essentially, they would be forced to side with China against their fellow Central Asians or, if groups in Ferghana or the mountains of southern Kazakstan were involved, against their own citizens. The murders of suspected Uighur activists in Bishkek in 2000 have made some Central Asians nervous about government loyalties to China. Just as the incidents of conflict in Ferghana have set the Central Asian governments against one another, so too might China's direct involvement in any related scenario (not necessarily in Ferghana itself) presage a wider conflict, even though that would be the last thing China's leaders want.

Iran's Ambivalence

Unlike China, Iran has ethnic and cultural ties to the eastern half of Central Asia, but few, apart from a deepening energy relationship with Kazakstan, are due to geography. Its principal Central Asian border is with Turkmenistan, and it is separated from Ferghana by hundreds of miles of foreign territory. In addition, the vast majority of Central Asian Muslims are Sunni, not Shi'a. Of the regional factors that interest Iranian leaders, a role in Ferghana lags behind Caspian development and positive relations with Russia. However, both of those interests have been complicated by persistent conflict in this part of Central Asia, while many Iranians still feel sympathy for the fate of their ethnic cousins, the Tajiks.[28]

The problem for Iran is that its sense of cultural kinship has only in few instances been reciprocated. Instead, most regional governments have been more interested in commercial ties. Kazakstan has maintained cordial relations with Iran despite differences over the Caspian Sea delimitation because the Kazak government hopes to capitalise in other areas, namely in sales of grain, electricity and metals.[29] Most Uzbek agricultural goods that do not go to Russia are exported via Turkmenistan to the Iranian port of Bandar Abbas. Turkmenistan places a high priority on good neighbourly relations with Iran, and has improved its southern transport and energy links.

Tajikistan, despite the Persian roots of its titular nationality, is relatively remote from Iran, and offers the fewest commercial opportunities. Tajikistan's interest and affinity with Iran is more complex than its status as the only non-Turkic Central Asian nation. Firstly, the Tajiks may be Persian, but unlike the Azeris nearly all are Sunni, and see little reason to make common cause with Iran's Shi'i theocracy simply because of a shared ethnic heritage. Next, in addition to doing what it can to keep out of the war in Afghanistan, the principal motive for the Tajik government in seeking allies is its concern about Uzbekistan. However, Iran's balanced regional policy rules it out as a protector of Tajikistan against Tashkent. Despite cool Iranian–Uzbek relations, Iran has too much to gain from cooperating with the Uzbeks in Afghanistan and combating Sunni radicalism generally to antagonise the Uzbek government by increasing its patronage of Tajiks.

Finally, Iran's relationship with both states is linked to the role it played in the Tajik civil war. Here, Tehran's relations with the Tajik IRP were not nearly as fraternal as some in the West and Russia made them out to be. Although key IRP leaders spent their exile in Iran during the civil war, others did so in Pakistan and Afghanistan, and established stronger ties there. Upon their return to Tajikistan and integration into the government, their primary focus was with consolidating a domestic political base by bolstering their nationalist credentials and addressing relations with Uzbekistan. When asked about Iran, prominent leaders of the reconstituted UTO often say they prefer to cultivate a 'good friend close to home rather than a distant relative'.[30] Neither Iran's Revolutionary Guards nor other groups have seriously opposed the Iranian Foreign Ministry's approach towards Tajikistan, unlike its policies in Afghanistan, Lebanon and elsewhere.[31] Thus, the IRP's ambivalence towards Iran is reflected by the stance of Iran towards most of Central Asia and the Caucasus.

This hands-off approach will, however, become impossible to sustain if tension in the Ferghana valley becomes more closely linked to developments in Afghanistan, where Iran has far more serious interests, or to a more active Iranian policy towards the South Caucasus. In Afghanistan, Iran has supported the anti-*Taliban* Northern Alliance, specifically ethnic Tajik leader Ahmed Shah Massoud. So long as Massoud relies on supply routes through Tajikistan and Uzbekistan, there is a risk that the Afghan conflict could spill over to the north. If Islamic militants in the Ferghana valley seriously threatened either the Uzbek or Tajik governments, or if support from international Muslim networks transformed any one of the Central Asian states into a sanctuary for anti-Shi'a groups, Iran's position could harden. Its early backing for Namangoni and Iranian intelligence activity throughout Central Asia suggest that elements in the Iranian government wish to establish or preserve some influence over the Sunni Islamists.[32] Iranian state radio has consistently broadcast favourable reports of militants' aims, for example claiming during the August 2000 crisis that they merely requested the release of all IMU prisoners, the reopening of mosques, freedom of religious expression and the introduction of Islamic law.[33]

Russia's Temptation

If scores are measured in prestige rather than actual costs, Russia has emerged as the key beneficiary of both the Tajik civil war and the Ferghana disturbances. Russia alone was able to bring peace to Tajikistan through its strong support for the Rakhmonov government, and its willingness to broker an agreement with the UTO and to allow the UN a significant presence on the ground during implementation. Despite ample rhetoric from regional governments about the menace Russia posed to their independence, all turned principally to Moscow for help during and after the Batken incidents in 1999 and 2000.

Russian officials responded with little hesitation. Although the threat from Central Asian Islamic militants was described at the time as a mere 'headache' by former Russian Defence Minister Igor Sergeyev, the government used the opportunity to reactivate its ties with Central Asian security forces.[34] Russia has reinvigorated CIS military activities to a degree not seen in over five years. In February 2000, the first phase of the 'Southern Shield 2000' exercise took place near Dushanbe with Kazak, Kyrgyz, Russian, Tajik and Uzbek troops, the largest military exercise in Central Asia since independence. This was followed by smaller exercises in each state, as well as a CIS air-defence exercise under the command of Lieutenant-General Yuri Bondarev, the deputy chief of the Russian air forces and commander of the CIS Joint Air Defence System. Separate bilateral exercises were conducted under Russian supervision with Ukraine and Uzbekistan, neither of which had formally been part of the CIS Joint Air Defence.

These activities demonstrate not only a renewed Russian commitment to CIS security, but also confirm that the Central Asian militaries have not severed all ties with their Russian counterparts, and do not intend to back with force their governments' occasionally strident anti-Russian rhetoric. This is true with regard to basic strategic orientation, as well as for everything from supply networks to training. The head of operations for the Uzbek army, Colonel Adbusattar Karimkulov, stated in 1997 that 'we have no desire to replace perfectly good Soviet doctrine we were brought up on with something else entirely. We'll simply acquire pieces of what suits us'.[35] In December 1999, Karimov, previously the most adamant about his country's break with Russia and its pro-Western leanings, voiced his support for a 'strategic alliance' with Russia to combat terrorism.[36] A high-profile visit by Putin in May 2000 and the signing of over 30 bilateral agreements led many observers to conclude that Uzbekistan had returned to the Russian fold, despite the Uzbek government's insistence that the shift was merely a temporary measure brought about by necessity. Later in 2000, the Karimov regime did indeed take a different tack, seeking reconciliation with the *Taliban* in an effort to cut off its support for the IMU, while denouncing Russian policies in the region. Coming years are likely to see many more such twists and turns as regimes struggle for survival.

One pattern that is likely to endure is the way that regional governments use security threats as opportunities to enhance their status relative to one another. The Uzbek government in particular has usually preferred to oppose Russian or CIS-sponsored actions, particularly when they put Uzbekistan on an equal footing with Kazakstan, Kyrgyzstan and Tajikistan; but it has also been happy to cooperate with Russia when doing so suited Uzbek interests, namely when it implied a condominium with Uzbekistan as an equal partner. Neither stance has reassured the other Central Asian states. Kazakstan and Kyrgyzstan have their own ethnic, geographic and economic reasons for maintaining strong and positive relations with Russia, and each has tried to avoid confusing these with competition with Uzbekistan for Russian favour. The Rakhmonov government in Tajikistan has remained something of a puppet regime by virtue of the presence in the country of the former Soviet 201st motorised rifle division and Russian border guards, which have not only kept the Kulobis in power, but have also managed the regional arms and narcotics trade from Afghanistan in ways that augment the government's authority, since it has no better means of controlling its southern frontier.[37]

Russian attempts to manipulate its tactical alliance with Uzbekistan or any other state could backfire if regional tensions escalate into open rivalry. Russian leaders may hope to preserve some freedom of manoeuvre in the former empire, but Russia's economic weakness makes for a deep reluctance to incur heavy new costs. Many Russians recall Soviet Russian stereotypes of avaricious and crafty Central Asians inventing new ways to extract resources from Russia. An indefinite and unilateral Russian security burden in Ferghana, leading to serious casualties, would alienate many Chechnya-weary Russians. A more aggressive presence throughout Central Asia would ultimately risk provoking counter-moves by other major powers, particularly the US, and jeopardise relations with China and Iran.

Outcomes

The most noteworthy feature of the conflicts involving Ferghana has been their incongruity with the neat set of international rivalries posited by many Western analysts. As Olivier Roy summarises:

> *The problem for the Islamist movements in developing a regional strategy is to find allies. For that, they have to take into account the complexity of the strategic landscape: the strategic interests of Uzbekistan (in the Tajik civil war) ran counter to that of Russia, but both claim to fight against the 'Islamic threat'; Iran is a strategic partner of Russia, while the main supporters of the Afghan Taliban are Pakistan and Saudi Arabia, two countries closely allied with the United States that have declared Usama bin Laden public enemy number one. The different set of alliances does not fit well together.*[38]

In Ferghana, as in Karabakh and Afghanistan, the governments of China, Iran, Russia and the US have been unable to transfer a familiar set of strategic tools to an unfamiliar environment. For the US in particular, its three main stated ambitions – democratisation, limiting the spread of Islamic radicalism, and containing Russian and Iranian influence – became mutually incompatible. In the case of democratisation and human rights, US goals have also been unacceptable to regional leaders. Their response has been further attempts at manipulation of other major powers. The Uzbek government in particular has tried to use its relationships with Russia and the US, these countries' presumed rivalry and the fear both have of Islamic radicalism, to gain the maximum advantage over both domestic and regional adversaries. The Tajik, Kyrgyz and Kazak governments have done the same with respect to China and Russia. The geopolitical misconceptions of the US and other powers suggest that they could be sucked into the region by local forces, without fully deciding or knowing what their hopes, goals, interests or policies actually are.

The real state of affairs in Central Asia is not one of rival imperial interests. It has more to do with banditry, territorial or socio-economic dislocation and relatively small-scale contests for land and resources. While it is true that much of this activity crosses borders, it does not do so in a way that directly affects the prestige or interests of the major powers. The possibility that these powers may be drawn into indirect or direct conflict with one another, either by lending support to a regional client or by playing too prominent a role themselves, is increased by the growing tendency to internationalise conflicts in this part of the world. The Afghan case that follows provides the clearest example of where this kind of outside involvement can lead: a seemingly endless cycle of war, the effect of which has been to magnify the threat the situation itself actually poses in Central Asia, and beyond.

Chapter 4

Afghanistan

Afghanistan is where the regional story begins and ends. For many Cold War chroniclers, the Soviet withdrawal in 1989 set in motion the dissolution of the Union itself. Today, nearly every transnational problem in Central Eurasia is linked to the Afghan civil war, while the country's example has reinforced the perception of instability throughout Central Eurasia. The ruling *Taliban* and its guest, exiled Saudi terrorist Osama bin Laden, admit to supporting Chechen rebels, and Afghanistan recognises Chechen independence. They also provide fighters for the Pakistani-backed revolt in Kashmir, and sanctuary for terrorists from as far afield as Xinjiang, the Philippines, Yemen and Indonesia. And they threaten the states to their north with a regional drug war. Meanwhile, Afghanistan remains the world's favourite country for superlatives: the longest-running civil conflict, the largest number of refugees, the leading source of opium, the greatest number of landmines, the most extreme form of Islamic rule and, potentially, the world's most severe famine.

Afghanistan is a 'worst-case' template for Central Eurasia as a whole. It encapsulates a number of regional themes, among them the extreme failure of a client state; the direct relationship between domestic instability in neighbouring states and the perception of a conflict 'spreading' across frontiers; and the consequences of diplomatic neglect by distant powers like the US, whose half-hearted actions have served only to help make the country a pariah. Like all its neighbours, Afghanistan is a diverse and difficult territory that

Map 4 Afghanistan

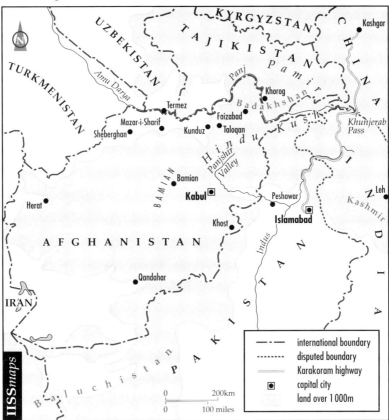

cannot be ruled effectively by an outside power, or by one of the country's component ethnic or tribal groups. In turn, ungovernability has attracted greater outside interference to contain, manage or profit by it.

Background

Afghanistan's endemic divisions have attracted outside intervention since the first empires appeared in Asia, vitiating the notion of a single state during nearly all of Afghan history.[1] After the Soviet defeat, however, the Afghan tragedy re-acquired a global dimension. This is partly the result of the ease with which narcotics, small arms and radical ideology now transit the world; and partly because of the growing threat the war poses to the interests of Iran, Pakistan, Russia, India and China, and its capacity to drive them into deeper conflict with one another, and with the US.

The Setting

For centuries, Afghanistan has been both a conduit and an obstacle for rival outside powers – Turkic, Persian and Mongol.[2] Situated between China, India, Pakistan, Iran and the three Central Asian republics of Turkmenistan, Uzbekistan and Tajikistan, Afghanistan is a borderland not only between the Middle East and South Asia, but also between the Transoxianan desert on one northern side, the Pamirs on the other, and the Indian subcontinent below. The predominant internal feature is the Hindu Kush range, which separates the country along a north-easterly axis. Thus, like its northern neighbours, Afghanistan suffers the twin geographic curses of sitting astride powerful nations, and having sharp internal, physical divisions.

Afghanistan's population is a legacy of its history. The south is mostly Pushtun, and the north home to Tajiks, Uzbeks, Hazaras (descendants of Mongol invaders and now predominantly Shi'a) and numerous other groups, ranging from Turkmen tribes along the north-western border to Baluch in the south-west and the descendants of Alexander's Macedonians in remote Nuristan. Within each ethnic group, there are additional divisions of tribe, region and class.[3]

The Trajectory of War since 1989

The Soviet withdrawal in 1988–89 concluded a chaotic decade of resistance, and set the stage for civil war between the 'resistance' forces.[4] Throughout the Soviet occupation, Pakistan's Inter-Services Intelligence (ISI) Directorate, the CIA and the Iranian government were all involved in equipping these forces. Pakistani field operatives, in particular, were reported to dictate everything, from the opening and closing of roads and the sale and purchase of commodities to the brokering of alliances among local commanders. At its peak, combined military assistance from the US and Saudi Arabia ran to about $1bn per year.[5] However, with the withdrawal of

Soviet troops official external assistance largely dried up. The US and Saudi Arabia abandoned much of their armed network in Afghanistan, while the relationship between the ISI, Iran and the principal commanders became more complicated, and more strained.[6]

Within Afghanistan, the picture became still more confused as the Soviet-installed government of Ahmedzai Najibullah and the state itself collapsed under the pressure of long-standing ethnic divisions and the vacuum created by the withdrawal of external support. In March 1990, Defence Minister Shahnawaz Tanai (a Khalqi and Pushtun) staged a coup attempt against Najibullah. Defeated, he fled to Pakistan and joined forces with Gulbuddin Hikmatyar, one of the most powerful Pushtun guerrilla leaders during the Soviet occupation and, despite his known anti-Americanism, a major recipient of Pakistani, Saudi and US military largesse. Hikmatyar rejected an interim government under Najibullah, while further splits emerged between Saudi-, Pakistani- and Iranian-based exile groups.[7]

Najibullah's government soon fell. Ahmed Shah Massoud (a Tajik former engineering student and legendary guerrilla leader in the Panjshir Valley), Uzbek commander Abdul Rashid Dostum, the leader of the then-formidable Jowzjan militia, and the Hazara-led *Hizb-i Wahdat* were left in control of Kabul. They would form the kernel of what would later be known as the 'Northern Alliance'. A new government under the Tajik opposition leader Burhanuddin Rabbani was announced, which included representatives of all three groups, as well as members of the defeated regime. Hikmatyar and most Ghilzai Pushtuns were excluded, and immediately began shelling the capital. After intervention by King Fahd of Saudi Arabia, a new accord was signed that brought Hikmatyar, now allied temporarily with the *Hizb-i Wahdat*, into the government as prime minister. Massoud refused to surrender any of his power as defence minister, the arrangement broke down and Hikmatyar and Dostum's forces shelled the city anew. As the war in the capital continued and each commander strengthened his grip over his regional base (Massoud in the Panjshir; Dostum in the north around Mazar-i-Sharif; and prominent local commander Ismail Khan in Herat), 1994 saw an interesting new group form in the south. It called itself the *Taliban*.

The *Taliban*'s leadership comprised Pushtuns from Qandahar, then a mainly warlord-controlled no-man's-land. Groups of students, or *Talibs*, began to organise to combat this lawlessness, and drew a steady stream of young recruits from the local *madrassas* and refugee camps across the border in Pakistan. They rapidly attracted the attention of the Pakistani government, which had become impatient with Hikmatyar and other Pushtun leaders. The decision was taken to enlist the nascent *Taliban* in a scheme to open a road from Pakistan to Herat and on to Turkmenistan, thereby giving Islamabad a highway to Central Asia. Agreement was reached with Ismail Khan, and the *Taliban* began to receive significant support from Pakistan. The new programme was rumoured to be the brainchild of former Pakistani Interior Minister Naseerullah Babar, himself Pushtun, who had convinced Prime Minister Benazir Bhutto and a reluctant military to distance themselves from Hikmatyar. Contrary to later stereotypes, the movement was not conceived as an attempt to reassert Pushtun dominance over the entire country, but rather to bring some order to the south, and to help disengage the Pakistani army from its reliance on Hikmatyar.[8]

With Pakistani help, the *Taliban* swept across the country with remarkable speed, capturing Qandahar and the surrounding 12 provinces by March 1995. Ismail Khan was defeated, and Herat conquered in September. Jalalabad was taken by the following July, and Kabul by September. The *Taliban* was in control of over half of Afghan territory, including areas beyond the traditional Pushtun homelands. In late 1996, the *Taliban* took its campaign to the north, and in May 1997 briefly captured Dostum's stronghold of Mazar-i-Sharif. The city changed hands in late 1997, before the *Taliban* retook it in May 1998. Dostum fled into exile. That September, Hazara commanders in Bamian were defeated. In 2000, the *Taliban* continued its advance into Massoud's core territory, capturing the important northern town of Taloqan.[9] *Taliban* advances were so impressive that rumours circulated towards the end of August that Russian officials had initiated secret talks with its leadership, while France signalled that it might be willing to become the first European country to grant the *Taliban* official recognition.[10] Uzbek overtures followed. By the end of 2000, the *Taliban* controlled about 95% of the country, and the defeat or marginalisation of Massoud, now its sole opponent in the north, appeared imminent. Yet he amassed reinforcements throughout the winter, while in April 2001 Dostum was reported to have returned to the country, which some observers took to foreshadow a new spring offensive under a reunited Northern Alliance.

The standard Western view of the Afghan war since the consolidation of the *Taliban* in 1996 has been of a largely north–south fight between Pushtuns and non-Pushtuns. But unlike the Karabakh situation or the flare-ups in Ferghana, the Afghan conflict is not *chiefly* a domestic struggle among ethnic or regionally-based clans for territorial and economic advantage, with international actors playing an occasionally critical role. Rather, it is unmistakably an internationalised civil war. Iran, Pakistan, Russia, Tajikistan and Uzbekistan have all been involved in furthering it, but none of these states has fully managed the consequences of its involvement.[11] By 1997, their governments believed that the Afghan war posed a direct and serious threat to regional peace. Ethnic and historic alliances provided motives for interference that were often as complex as those of the warring parties themselves.

Pakistan's Ambition

Pakistan has played a central role in the Afghan conflict, both in supporting the *mujaheddin* against the Soviet occupation and in transforming the *Taliban* into a military force. Pakistan's regional ambitions were not, however, the decisive factor in either initiative. Islamabad is certainly interested in building 'strategic depth' by way of its Afghan clients, which at least two generations of Pakistani strategists have taken to mean an indirect attempt to counter Indian hegemony in South Asia, and tilt the balance of power in Kashmir. But given Islamabad's frustrations in both Afghanistan and Kashmir, 'strategic depth' is probably more strategic fiction than fact.

Deeper analysis suggests that Pakistan's involvement has had important domestic and ideological rationales. It has had a strong internal function, namely preventing a revival of Pushtun nationalism, both at home and in Afghanistan. This has long preoccupied Pakistan's non-Pushtun leaders and, particularly in the 1970s, strained relations between the two countries.[12] Among many liberal Pakistanis, there also persisted the basic desire to export dissent in order to divert the energies of political opponents, especially in the increasingly powerful religious parties. As Pakistan became more

Islamicised under Zia ul-Haq in the 1980s, these parties, especially the *Jama'at-i Islami* and the *Jami'at-e Ulema Islam* (JUI), became more prominent, necessitating a direct role for them in the *jihad* against the Soviet occupation of Afghanistan.[13] The Soviet withdrawal gave them no reason to cease their efforts. Nor was their continued activism discouraged by their former American comrades in arms. Islamic radicalism in any event was perceived by ambitious Afghans like Hikmatyar to be the 'wave of the future', and Afghanistan, for better or worse, gave it fertile ground in which to prosper.

By the late 1990s, Pakistan's forward policy in Afghanistan had begun to backfire. The dramatic increases in drug use, arms and contraband smuggling and related corruption had been poisoning the domestic environment in Pakistan since the death of Zia in 1988, but the scale was now reaching alarming levels. Pakistan is home to an estimated three million heroin addicts, perhaps the world's highest number.[14] Of still greater concern to liberal Pakistani élites was the renewed appeal of Sunni radicalism, creating a perceived threat of what some observers have called the 'Talibanisation' of Pakistan: its transformation into a theocratic and anti-modern country. While this danger remains distant at present, by the end of the 1990s it had become commonplace in the West to speak of Pakistan as on the way to becoming the first 'failed' nuclear state.[15]

Pakistan's priority has been to contain the ill-effects of the Afghan war, or at least to exert some control over them. This has proved increasingly difficult for General Pervez Musharraf's military government, which seized power in October 1999. Musharraf has neither been able to dictate policy to the Pakistani Islamic parties whose support he needed to gain power, nor fully to manage the *Taliban*. Thus, his policy has followed the same incremental line of his predecessors, Bhutto and Nawaz Sharif. Support for the *Taliban*, though not as considerable as in the 1990s, has continued.

Pakistani officials continue to cite Pakistan's alleged 'encirclement' by India, Iran and Russia as an excuse for Pakistani involvement in Afghanistan.[16] This Pakistani rhetoric in turn has encouraged these three states to support the Northern Alliance in an effort to restrain Pakistani influence in Afghanistan, and hence in Central Asia. This rivalry also led Pakistan to try to encourage the US to support its role in Afghanistan. In particular, Islamabad urged

Washington to consider the possibility of a gas pipeline from Turkmenistan through Afghanistan and Pakistan to the Arabian Sea, thereby bypassing both Iran and Russia. The threat of this (though it was never a realistic scheme at the time) was cited by some Western observers as giving Russia and Iran a motive to prolong Afghan fighting in order to make the pipeline impossible.[17] Enemies of the *Taliban* have also suggested that Pakistan, as the ally of Saudi Arabia and the principal conduit and beneficiary of Saudi largesse to Afghan factions, was acting as the Arab world's forward agent in Central Asia. Yet bin Laden's presence in Afghanistan ended official Saudi underwriting of the *Taliban* in 1998, and Saudi missionary activity throughout Central Asia had already been curtailed. In October 1999, UN Resolution 1267 imposed sanctions on the *Taliban* for its failure to hand over bin Laden, and in February 2001 *Taliban* authorities expelled the UN from Kabul. In these circumstances, a positive official Arab view of Pakistan's support for the *Taliban* became impossible to sustain.

Now the sole international supporter of the *Taliban*, Pakistan began to feel the weight of its many sectarian and ethnic troubles at home, and hardly needed to reinvent itself as the regional defender of hardline Sunni interests. Given both the internal threat of Sunni radicalism in Pakistan and the danger of US sanctions, Pakistan's own long-term stability is not consistent with such a role – a conclusion reached by the Pakistani government at the end of the 1990s. However, Pakistan's room for manoeuvre against the *Taliban* has remained limited by the fact that Afghanistan is a major player in Pakistan's own domestic politics. Pakistan cannot withdraw from Afghanistan altogether, because of the threat to its own stability from both religious radicalism and Pushtun nationalism. It therefore has to go on trying to influence the *Taliban* in a positive direction.

The significant population of Baluchis in Pakistan, Afghanistan and Iran poses a further set of challenges for Islamabad. Any direct clash with Iran would increase the possibility of Baluch irredentist activity within Pakistan.[18] The Pakistani motive for involvement in Afghanistan also holds true for splits among Pushtuns there, and in Pakistan's North-West Frontier Province. Maintaining some measure of balance has been difficult for Islamabad. The fragmentation of Afghanistan since 1989 has reinforced distinctions between groups, the intra-Pushtun Durrani/ Ghilzai split being the best known, and encouraged frequent shifts of allegiance.[19] Thus, not only are Tajik and Uzbek Afghans presumed to be fighting on behalf of their kinsmen across the border, as well as for Russia and Iran, but so too are Hazaras (on behalf of fellow Shi'a) and disaffected Pushtuns, who have competed against one another for most-favoured treatment from Pakistan. This has put the Pakistani sponsors of the Afghan war in a difficult position, at odds not only with many of the factions they sought to help, but also with the presumed sponsors of those they sought to hurt.

Iran's Lament

Officials in Tehran certainly suspected a sectarian motive when the *Taliban* re-entered Mazar-i-Sharif in August 1998 and executed several diplomats and journalists seeking refuge in the Iranian consulate. Within weeks, Iran had mobilised some 200,000 troops along the eastern border, and an invasion appeared imminent. None took place, largely as a result of eleventh-hour diplomacy by UN envoy Lakhdar Brahimi and some clear thinking in Iran about the longer-term ramifications of occupying Herat and large parts of western Afghanistan. This would have involved enormous costs and drawn Iran directly into conflict with the *Taliban* and, by extension, with Pakistan, and possibly with radical Sunnis throughout the Arab world.

Iran's response to the executions was more a result of outrage and frustration than it was part of a broader strategy. Iran's policy in Afghanistan has been consistent with its cautious but fragmented approach towards Central Asia and the Caucasus as a whole. Despite hosting several thousand Afghan refugees during the Soviet occupation, Iran was isolated from the principal networks of *mujaheddin* support, and had little leverage within Afghanistan once the Soviets withdrew. It defined its interests as protecting Afghan Shi'a, and searching for ways to return the refugees who remained on its side of the border.

As the civil war progressed, however, Iran grew more concerned that an outright *Taliban* victory would destabilise its eastern border, and possibly enhance Pakistan's (and what it imagined to be Saudi Arabia's) position in the Middle East. Cooperation with Russia in other areas extended to Afghanistan and, following the *Taliban* victories of 1996 and 1997 and the 1998 consulate incident, Iran put itself firmly on the side of the Northern Alliance. In so doing, Iran's mullahs were likely to feel as little cultural obligation towards the Afghan Tajiks or other Farsi-speakers as they did towards the Tajiks of Tajikistan: with the exception of the Hazara Shi'a of central Afghanistan, they were distant, largely Sunni, cousins, and neither willing nor dependable surrogates.

Besides increasing concern over the flow of drugs from Afghanistan, Tehran's primary goal became to contain what it saw as Pakistani adventurism that threatened Iran's status as the main north–south corridor between Central Asia and the Middle East. Iran's clerics were also seized by a fear of Sunni radicalism. In addition to the activities of Pakistani religious associations, Afghanistan is home to the 'Arab Afghans', volunteers who had joined the anti-Soviet *jihad*, and later made the country the capital of international terrorism. By the end of the 1990s, these militants, bin Laden among them, had become the new heroes of the Sunni dispossessed. But here again, Iran's purpose in resisting this activity is as much part of its aim to balance the perceived regional influence of Pakistan and Saudi Arabia as it is to advance the appeal of any theology, or to bolster conservative positions at home.[20]

Thus, Iran has been cautious, quietly asserting its interests, but not in pursuit of a clear policy aimed at creating a regional ally. Iran has been one of the more active members of the UN's 'six-plus-two' consultative arrangement for Afghanistan, which comprises the four border states plus Russia and the US. As with Karabakh and Tajikistan, it has also promoted good-faith attempts to mediate. Tehran has no interest in seeing the disintegration of Pakistan for fear of the boost this might give to Baluch nationalism at home or in Pakistan. Even worse would be an alliance between Pushtun and Baluch nationalists against their Persian and Punjabi or Sindi masters in either state. This possibility gave rise to considerable concern in the 1970s, and may resurface if Afghanistan remains seriously or permanently divided between Pushtun and non-Pushtun factions.[21]

Iran will continue to compete marginally with Pakistan by supporting opposing forces in the Afghan war, but is unlikely to risk war with Pakistan on behalf of its Afghan clients. So long as war continues there, Iran may benefit just as marginally from Pakistan's over-exertion in Afghanistan as it did from Turkey's in the South Caucasus. But continued conflict is not in Iran's ultimate interest, particularly if it compels more aggressive Iranian behaviour in the region, a prospect that many Central Asians quietly fear.[22]

The Asian Connection

Afghanistan has increasingly figured in Chinese and Indian thinking as well, but as yet without any major practical impact in Afghanistan itself. Leaders in Beijing and New Delhi see the Afghan war as an important part of their evolving triangular relationship with Pakistan, and both share common concerns over transnational threats. China sent a delegation to meet *Taliban* leaders in March 1999, while India cautiously supported the Northern Alliance. At the same time, both countries hoped for peace.

Instability in Afghanistan is damaging to India domestically because it is preventing the construction of north–south gas pipelines, which India hopes will complement others from Iran and Russia.[23] Afghanistan's war economy is fuelling India's profligate opium market, while links are expanding between militant groups in Afghanistan and those still threatening Indian forces in Kashmir. India in coming years is bound to become more directly involved in Central Asia, in order to balance its growing dependence on Gulf and East Asian sources of energy and in pursuit of its own brand of strategic depth, though its officials deny any specific interest in projecting power northwards.[24]

Concerns over resistance activity in Xinjiang and Tibet inform China's views of Afghanistan. There is almost no evidence that China has sought to become involved in Afghanistan (or anywhere else in Central Asia) in order to minimise Indian influence or thwart its ambitions, despite common borders with both countries and contrary attitudes in India.[25] China's restrictions on movement across its borders, its pressure on Islamabad to curtail Pakistan-based missionaries and its overtures to the *Taliban* all suggest that Beijing seeks to contain a threat from Afghanistan through a combination of constraint and accommodation, rather than opposition. But if unrest by Uighurs trained in Afghanistan increases, China's leadership could be prompted into deeper involvement.

American and Russian Antipathy

Both Russia and the US kept their distance from Afghanistan during the 1990s. The US interest in Afghanistan diminished radically following the Soviet withdrawal and, despite attempts to engage the various Afghan parties, including the *Taliban* in 1996, and passing interest in trans-Afghan pipelines, Washington assigned a low priority to what its diplomats considered a hopeless situation. Only by the end of the decade, following the bombing of its embassies in Kenya and Tanzania and the subsequent missile attack on bin Laden's Afghan bases in August 1998, did the US begin to show renewed strategic interest. It has frequently been suggested that the US is the only major power capable of ending the Afghan war.[26] But a more serious level of engagement would require a change of policy and considerable public education about US interests there. Neither appears likely given the growing friendship between the US and India in the wake of Clinton's April 2000 visit to South Asia, and the complex nature of US policies towards the military regime in Pakistan. For better or worse, the US government has concluded that the burden is on Pakistan to repair the damage that it has helped to cause across the border.

Russian leaders meanwhile feel a still-deeper aversion towards Afghanistan. Just as it took the US decades to come to terms with its defeat in Vietnam, an 'Afghan syndrome' still plagues Russia. But the country does not have an ocean between itself and Afghanistan, and its history of involvement dates back to the early nineteenth century. Thus, Afghanistan, specifically the *Taliban*, has become part of the anti-Islamist crusade that Russia under Putin has defined for itself as a principal strategic vocation in the country's unstable south. Russia has continued to support the Northern Alliance, including the Soviets' former nemesis Massoud, and has encouraged the entrenchment and enrichment of Russian border guards along the Tajik–Afghan frontier.

Russia's Afghan involvement was also linked to its use of 'the Tajik card' in relations with Uzbekistan since 1994. Its leaders concurred with their Uzbek counterparts that the threat posed by the fall of Mazar-i-Sharif did not stem from any likelihood that hordes of crazed *Taliban* fundamentalists would cross the border. Although the Uzbek government drew a dire picture of the Islamist threat, it had other concerns. If the *Taliban* succeeded in defeating Massoud, his heavily-armed forces would almost certainly cross into Tajikistan. Even if they did not transform the south of the country into an anti-*Taliban* stronghold, their presence would further upset the delicate balance of ethnic power in Tajikistan, from which Uzbekistan's clients in Khujand had been excluded at the behest of the Russian-backed Kulobi faction. Nearly three years after the panic resulting from the *Taliban*'s northern conquests, this fear has remained at the centre of Uzbek concerns over Afghanistan, and key to the Russian government's thinking as well. A large-scale migration of Uzbeks from Tajikistan into Uzbekistan is not far-fetched; and a resulting ethnic panic among Tajiks in Uzbekistan, who make up a sizeable portion of the population of Samarkand and Bukhara, could threaten the balkanisation of everywhere south of Kazakstan.[27] In the view of Tashkent and Moscow, Massoud had to be helped at all costs to maintain his position in Afghanistan.

For Russia's strategists, the priority since 1997 has been to keep the Rakhmanov government and the peace accord alive in Tajikistan.[28] Thus, helping the Tajiks in Afghanistan in order to forestall a human crisis on the border was in Russia's interest, as was keeping the pressure on the *Taliban* to minimise its ability to provide succour to those fighting Russia in the north Caucasus. However, Russia was careful to act in ways that did not grant any additional leverage to Uzbekistan, which had staked a claim as regional leader. This role did not necessarily offend Russian interests *per se*, but rather caused problems for its allies, particularly in Tajikistan and Kyrgyzstan.

Thus, in May 2000 Russian border guards in Tajikistan allowed the evacuation of an estimated 400 of Namangoni's militants across the border into Afghanistan to join the other anti-Karimov group of Tohir Yoldosh near Kunduz. Although leaders of different movements, Yoldosh and Namangoni shared similar origins – after the 1989–90 Namangan persecutions, Yoldosh joined the UTO, eventually becoming deputy to Abdullo Nuri, the chairman of the Tajik IRP and one of the post powerful men in

Tajikistan. The two also shared the same enemy: the Karimov regime in Tashkent. The May move was negotiated with Namangoni by the Tajik Minister of Emergencies Mirzo Zio, the former commander of UTO forces and ally of Yoldosh. Although a large portion of Namangoni's fighters remained in Tajikistan, and launched another incursion into Kyrgyz and Uzbek territory in August, the move to Afghanistan was seen to facilitate their ability to mobilise the support required to mount a direct attack on Uzbekistan, raising the prospect that Uzbekistan might launch pre-emptive raids on Namangoni's camps.[29] Reports circulated that Uzbek aircraft bombed northern Afghanistan several times, and that one was shot down in July. Uzbekistan has, however, abstained from intervening directly in the Afghan war, and Karimov has quietly expressed greater willingness to negotiate with the *Taliban* in the hope that its leaders will end their support for his enemies.

Providing a check on Uzbekistan was not Russia's only reason for playing 'the Tajik card' with regard to Afghanistan. Like their Iranian and Pakistani counterparts, Russian leaders throughout the 1990s believed that the prolongation of the war was preferable to outright victory for the side opposing the one they supported. Yet Pakistan's disintegration would be as unfavourable to Russia as the creation of a Pakistani client state in Afghanistan. In addition to the instability either would cause in Central Asia, a reconfiguration that resulted in too much power going to any single regional state would damage Russia's broader objectives in the Middle East and South Asia. Although rarely mentioned and considered fanciful by most Western experts, Russian objectives are still wedded to Soviet ambitions to check Western pre-eminence in the Gulf, for which Russia requires the freedom to manipulate regional powers.[30]

The Afghan Vortex

Central Asia cannot be truly stable so long as there is war in Afghanistan. And peace cannot come to Afghanistan so long as Central Asia itself is fundamentally unstable. This has been the conundrum at the heart of the Afghan tragedy.

Afghanistan has re-emerged as the central staging area for Central Asia's most salient conflicts: sectarian, ethnic, socio-economic and ideological. It has demonstrated the capacity for unrest of large uprooted or marginalised populations, present nearly everywhere in Central Asia and the Caucasus, from the thousands of refugees in squalid camps in Azerbaijan to hundreds of internally-displaced Uighurs in Xinjiang. In such environments, extreme ideologies flourish and become uncontrollable, even by their instigators. The ease with which the contained, proxy conflict in Afghanistan was transformed into an internationalised civil war has set a dangerous precedent for other regional states should they ever fall prey to the same degree of internal disintegration. Neighbouring powers that have sought to manage the chaos in Afghanistan have found that doing so requires more resources and stamina than they ultimately may be prepared to provide. But their interests in the region have been equally ill-served by doing little.

Unwilling to take full responsibility for their respective stakes in Afghanistan, the governments of the major powers have instead delegated authority within, and occasionally outside, their own official bureaucracies to junior subordinates with inadequate experience, narrow biases and limited responsibilities. Thus, while regional regimes have grown more centralised, the governments of the major powers have become more decentralised in their handling of regional matters. This has multiplied the ill-effects of what is now commonly termed 'blowback', thereby increasing the chances that each neighbouring power, in order to demonstrate its authority to the others as well as to its domestic constituencies, will undertake ventures such as sporadic missile strikes or covert assistance to warlords, which may not have direct relevance to ending the war, and may in fact escalate it. Put differently, 'instability in the internal politics of a buffer state can easily generate security dilemmas among neighbouring states, as each tries to assure that its rivals do not exploit the resulting opportunities'.[31] This mismatch between intent and capacity is made worse by the interwoven ethnic, geographic and historic links that have blurred the line between domestic and international consequences, and have come to prescribe the essence of wider regional conflict. The resulting burden on the major powers has merely increased, bringing to mind an observation of Robert Byron, who visited Afghanistan in 1934:

> *as far as I can see, the Russians were only doing what we do*
> *every year on the North-West Frontier: smothering tribal*
> *unrest before it could spread over the border ... If the Afghans*

> *can't keep their own house in order, the Russians will be*
> *liable to do it for them on the north, just as we do on the south*
> *... Naturally, the province's real safeguard lies in the fact*
> *that the Russians are not anxious to embroil themselves with*
> *the British, and that Afghanistan intact, if quiet, is useful to*
> *both Powers as a buffer. But the Afghans think it is*
> *humiliating to admit this ... Poor Asia! Everything boils*
> *down to the inevitable nationalism, the desire for self-*
> *sufficiency, the wish to cut a figure in the world and no*
> *longer be called interesting for lack of plumbing.*[32]

Outcomes

As long as the civil war in Afghanistan continues, the delicate balance between Uzbekistan and Tajikistan to its north will be threatened with serious disruption, just as Pakistan and Iran continue to cope with ever greater pressures to control their borders against refugees and smuggling. At the same time, a *Taliban* solution for Afghanistan, particularly if it excludes other groups, is bound to fail, and poses many of the same risks to neighbours as does prolonged war. Thus, Afghanistan's relevance to the rest of Central Eurasia has both symbolic and human dimensions. Projecting the image of Afghanistan onto the broader region as a future worst-case scenario can sound as far-fetched as the wild fears of a *Wahhabi* juggernaut driving to Samarkand, Bukhara and the Kazak steppe. But this scenario is not a fiction or mere symbol of gloom. It suggests analogies to other areas – Kashmir, for example – where major Eurasian powers have also fuelled internal conflicts, either directly or by failing to seize opportunities for addressing the deeper causes of conflict. These are more than boundary disputes or cultural battlegrounds. They involve actual demographic threats to the stability of borderlands and the internal balance of ethnic groups throughout the region.

For the major powers, the most relevant questions Afghanistan poses relate to the exercise of rivalry, rather than to its innate existence: can Iran, Pakistan, Russia and even the US get away with *not* intervening in proxy struggles, while professing the need to enforce a strategic 'balance' against one another? By contrast, do they really gain by persuading local actors to blur their aims with 'geopolitical' imperatives that markedly increase the rationale for conflict? To answer these questions one must look beyond Afghanistan, and weigh the efficacy of acts of 'punishment' against their costs, particularly for the US and its longer-term relations with Pakistan, Russia and the Gulf states. *Ad hoc* measures are obviously no substitute for the careful and difficult diplomacy required to rebuild a collapsed state, let alone to keep it from drawing its neighbours into anarchy. By the end of the decade, it had become clear to even the most hardline Americans that a policy built on so reactive and narrow a foundation would not succeed, even in restraining the activities of a single terrorist network. The problem was finding an alternative.

Conclusion

When it comes to realities on the ground, the disintegration of the Soviet Union has been more gradual than the dramatic events of 1989–91 would suggest. It began at least two decades beforehand, and continues today. Moscow no longer rules the other republics directly, but it still exerts considerable power. One reason for this is that – in contrast to the collapse of empires in the past – no outside power has stepped in with military force to replace Moscow's rule with its own.

The Soviet collapse has nonetheless been followed by an important reconfiguration of relationships, both within and among the new states. Internally, rulers have substituted new clan hierarchies for those favoured under Soviet rule, leading to the creation of more centralised regimes. The development of these clan-based autocracies has weakened the states concerned, and has in some cases worsened relations with others. Externally, with the exception of Karabakh there have been no clashes between states over territorial sovereignty. The insecure nationalist élites in the newly-independent states have on balance aimed to preserve control over their existing territory, rather than acquire more. Most of the regimes in the region believe, with good reason, that they are far more threatened by internal instability than by external aggression. Accordingly, relative restraint and flexibility are likely to persist. But given the relative decay of Russian power, the ambitions of other outside states and the underlying tensions between the regional countries themselves, this balance cannot be described as stable, and serious conflict will remain possible for the foreseeable future.

The most likely potential rivalries involve Iran, Turkey (backed to some extent by the US) and Russia in the South Caucasus; Iran and Pakistan, and possibly the Arab states, over Afghanistan (with limited involvement by the US and Russia); and China, Russia, India and Pakistan over one or more Central Asian states. The common feature of these potential clashes is that none need involve the West, or even the US. This is because real US interests are limited compared to those of the other major powers. Moreover, the entire region, including the South Caucasus, will be drawn towards greater involvement in the states to the south, rather than towards a distant and in most cases culturally alien Europe.

Russia and the US may continue to spar over Caspian resources. However, American difficulties in the Middle East, and growing rivalry with China, are likely to make geopolitical competition with Russia in Central Eurasia less significant to the US than its declaratory policy for much of the 1990s would seem to suggest. For that reason, Russo-centric policies in the region have ill-served regional stability and US national interests. US behaviour – heavily coloured by *Machtpolitik*, though without corresponding military commitments – has been a case-study of how a government can forget the overall rationale for policies. The saga of US support for the Baku–Ceyhan pipeline is one example of how what ought to be a single component of policy can become an end in itself, undermining or wrecking other goals. This approach has encouraged Russian responses which have also lost touch with Moscow's overall interest in regional stability. Instead, these responses have been dominated by the perceived need to combat US moves and weaken actual or would-be US allies like Georgia, Azerbaijan and Uzbekistan. The cumulative record of half-baked efforts by the US, Russia and others demonstrates the dangers of behaving in this way in a region where no outside power can be sure of controlling or limiting the impact of its actions.

Most US moves have genuinely been seen by their proponents as 'defensive' reactions to 'aggressive' moves by Russia – and precisely the same perception has driven Russian policy. Meanwhile, neither country has been willing or able to commit serious resources to stabilising the region under its hegemony. As the British historian Niall Ferguson has noted with regard to the outbreak of the First World War, it is most often weakness, not strength, which drives powers into conflict. This is usually by way of 'an extraordinary mixture of diplomatic and strategic commitment and practical and political non-commitment'.[1] The widespread belief among American 'Realists' in the inevitability of geopolitical contest might have been expected to decline with the end of the Cold War. This tendency has continued in part because of a continued assumption that Russia is an innately aggressive power, while its southern neighbours are cast as innocent 'victims'. This attitude has in turn resurrected the Communist-instilled belief among Russians (and Chinese) that the US is an innately 'imperialist' power. As the cases examined in this paper demonstrate, neither of these hostile images corresponds adequately to reality.

There is thus an urgent need to debunk the belief in inevitable strategic competition in Central Eurasia. A new understanding of the complexity of the region, and of outside interests there, could contribute to the creation of orderly and positive relations, both between the major powers and between the regional states themselves. Both are prerequisites for stability. But stability first requires some redefinition. The US promotion of rivalry in Central Eurasia in the name of stability commits the basic error of equating all geopolitics with power politics.[2] It encourages the national élites of the region to believe that the answer to their problems lies in the removal of certain outside influences, and the manipulation of outside rivalries, rather than in domestic reform and cooperation with their neighbours.

The question of whether peace can be achieved from within or must rely on the imposition of external hegemony is very much a false choice. As the decades-long agony of Afghanistan demonstrates, peace usually requires a mixture of internal reconciliation and agreement between the main outside players. The persistent mixture of local discord and external involvement also explains why the very different dispute in Karabakh remained unsettled despite a decade of peace efforts, some of which came very close to producing an agreement. This also helps us to understand why instability in Ferghana appears to grow worse by the year, despite the efforts of all five Central Asian states, as well as Russia, the US, Iran, Turkey and China, to reduce the damage caused by the insurgencies there. Brzezinski is clearly wrong in his conviction that 'the three grand imperatives of [US] imperial geostrategy are to prevent collusion and maintain security dependence among the vassals, to keep tributaries pliant and protected, and to keep the barbarians from coming together'.[3] Belief in this formula among both US and Russian policy-makers is precisely what has helped prolong or exacerbate instability in Central Eurasia. No regional state has the capacity to create stability for itself, but no single outside power or group of powers can unilaterally impose it.

By contrast, the idea of a 'concert of powers' pleases many geopolitically-minded but non-aggressive thinkers, who are attracted to models of international cooperation and stability based on an agreed 'equilibrium'. Whether this model can be applied to so fractious a region as Central Eurasia is, however, another question. For it to succeed, local states and outside powers will require a far greater consensus on aims and values. There is more to this than simply an agreement to cooperate. A successful concert also demands a sophisticated sensitivity among the major powers to each other's interests, as well as specifically-agreed deterrents to aggression.[4] Above all, outside states must recognise that instability within the region poses the greatest danger to all their interests. This insecurity can only be lessened by common and co-ordinated action, which relies in turn upon each power acting with regard for the legitimate interests of the others. Like its musical counterpart, a regional concert means the common organisation of diverse elements. This is extremely hard to achieve. Yet if any troubled region of the world offers opportunities for such an international concert, it is Central Eurasia. With the partial exception of Iran, no deep ideological conflict divides the great powers, least of all in this region. On the contrary, radical Sunni Islamist ideology as promoted by the *Taliban*, and the terrorism which it endorses, are a serious threat to them all, as is the proliferation of crime. If genuine geopolitical cooperation between Washington, Moscow, Beijing and Tehran cannot occur in this region, it is unlikely to occur anywhere, but a far more explicit multinational diplomatic effort is required for a regional concert to work. This would have to be initiated by the

US, and include, at a minimum, purposeful US accommodation with Iran, Russia and probably Pakistan. This should lead to a common focus on regional security threats, notably radical Islamism and militant activity associated with regional smuggling; and greater intelligence sharing to minimise them. If each external government wants to combat terrorism, promote stability and ensure for its people free and peaceful access to the region's resources – aims which they all endorse – then each must pursue these aims in concert with the other major powers. If, on the other hand, a US administration decided that its primary aim should be to establish semi-protectorates to limit the influence of other powers in the region, it would have to adopt a much more ruthless policy of power projection than has so far been the case. The attempt by the US to follow both approaches simultaneously helped unsettle the region, and encouraged similar responses from other major powers. It has become clear that hard decisions need to be taken in Washington about how important the region really is to the US, and what US interests there really are. This paper suggests that such thinking would conclude that true US interests in Central Eurasia do not differ profoundly from those of the powers hitherto seen as America's rivals, or even enemies.

Notes

Acknowledgements

The author would like to thank the many officials and scholars who contributed to this study, particularly C. Richard Nelson and Anatol Lieven.

Introduction

1 Roland Dannreuther, *Creating New States in Central Asia*, Adelphi Paper 288 (Oxford: Oxford University Press for the IISS, 1994).
2 Famously summarised in the maxim: 'Who rules East Europe commands the Heartland: Who rules the Heartland commands the World-Island: Who rules the World-Island commands the World.'
3 Zbigniew Brzezinski, *The Grand Chessboard: American Primacy and Its Geostrategic Imperatives* (New York: Basic Books, 1997), p. 39.
4 Stephen J. Blank, *US Military Engagement with Transcaucasia and Central Asia* (Carlisle Barracks, PA: US Army War College, June 2000), p. 5.

Chapter One

1 William Thompson, 'The Regional Subsystem: A Conceptual Explication and a Propositional Inventory', *International Studies Quarterly*, vol. 17, no. 1, March 1973, p. 93; Ian Bremmer, 'Southern Tier Subregionalism', *Perspectives on Central Asia*, July 1997.
2 Mohammad Reza-Djalili and Thierry Kellner, 'Moyen-Orient, Caucase et Asie Centrale: Des Concepts Géopolitiques à Construire et à Réconstruire', *Central Asian Survey*, vol. 19, no. 1, March 2000, pp. 117–40. The term 'inner Asia', popular with twentieth-century scholars like Owen Lattimore, has also been resurrected in *Central Asia: Crisis Conditions in Three States*, International Crisis Group, 7 August 2000.
3 For reasons unrelated to the region, India, Pakistan and Afghanistan were assigned to US Pacific Command, based in Hawaii, until 1998. Pakistan and Afghanistan, along with the five Central Asian states, are now

assigned to Central Command.

4 See Gerald Segal, *The Great Power Triangle* (London: Macmillan, 1982), pp. 4–8.

5 Dannreuther, *Creating New States in Central Asia*, pp. 3–4. For details of the transition in Armenia, see Edmund Herzig, *The New Caucasus: Armenia, Azerbaijan and Georgia* (London: Royal Institute of International Affairs, 1999), pp. 11–23.

6 Milan Hauner, *What Is Asia to Us? Russia's Asian Heartland Yesterday and Today* (London and New York: Routledge, 1992), pp. 22–48, 61–65. See also Irina Zviagelskaia, *The Russian Policy Debate on Central Asia* (London: Royal Institute of International Affairs, 1995); and Firuz Kazemzadeh, *Russia and Britain in Persia, 1864–1914* (New Haven, CT and London: Yale University Press, 1968), pp. 33ff.

7 Celeste A. Wallender, 'Russian National Security Policy in 2000', memo 102, Program on New Approaches to Russian Security, Davis Center for Russian Studies, Harvard University, Boston, MA; and John Erickson, 'Russia Will Not Be Trifled With: Geopolitical Facts and Fantasies', *Journal of Strategic Studies*, vol. 22, nos 2 and 3, June–September 1999, pp. 260–63.

8 'Governments Anticipate Renewed Outbreak of Islamic Militancy in the Spring', *Jamestown Monitor*, 4 February 2000.

9 Charles Clover, 'Dreams of the Eurasian Heartland', *Foreign Affairs*, vol. 78, no. 2, March–April 1999; Erickson, 'Russia Will Not Be Trifled With', pp. 242–68; and Hauner, *What Is Asia to Us?*, pp. 216–43.

10 Richard Pomfret, *Central Asia Turns South? Trade Relations in Transition* (London: Royal Institute of International Affairs, 1999), pp. 30–43.

11 *Tajikistan: Refugee Reintegration and Conflict Prevention* (New York: Forced Migration Project, Open Society Institute, 1998), pp. vi, 9.

12 Interview with Tara Kartha, Institute for Defence and Security Analysis, New Delhi, July 1998.

13 After being told of his appointment as foreign minister, Shikhmuradov spent several weeks in the state archives in Moscow and Tehran reading up on the last two centuries of those relations. Interview with Boris Shikhmuradov, Ashkabad, June 1997.

14 W. J. F. Jenner, *The Tyranny of History: The Roots of China's Crisis* (London: Allen Lane, 1992), p. 94; and Paul Wheatley, *The Pivot of the Four Corners: A Preliminary Enquiry Into the Origins and Character of the Ancient Chinese City* (Chicago, IL: Aldine Publishing Company, 1971), pp. 298–302, 411–19.

15 See Mahnaz Z. Ispahani, *Pakistan: Dimensions of Insecurity*, Adelphi Paper 246 (London: Brassey's for the IISS, 1989–90).

16 Speech by Hassan Rohani, Deputy Speaker of the Iranian parliament and Secretary of the High National Security Council, Institute for Political and International Studies, conference, Tehran, 25 January 2000.

17 For a critique of this view, see Robert Zoellick, 'Clinton's Last Chance to Get Russia Policy Right', *Wall Street Journal*, 27 March 2000.

18 Dan Morgan and David Ottaway, 'Pipe Dreams: The Struggle for Caspian Oil', *Washington Post*, 4–6 October 1998.

[19] Rajan Menon, 'Treacherous Terrain: The Political and Security Dimensions of Energy Development in the Caspian Sea Zone', *NBR Analysis*, vol. 9, no. 1, 1998, p. 11; Rosemary Forsythe, *The Politics of Oil in the Caucasus and Central Asia*, Adelphi Paper 300 (Oxford: Oxford University Press for the IISS, 1996), pp. 11–12, 37–43.

[20] US rhetoric never opposed eventual Iranian and Russian routes, but merely cast the issue as one of timing: if the Baku–Ceyhan did not take priority over other routes, the market would prevent a main export pipeline through Turkey from ever being built, whereas the others were sure to develop anyway.

[21] In November 2000, Wolf was replaced by Elizabeth Jones, former US ambassador to Kazakstan.

[22] About $10 billion-worth of contracts have been signed with Iran since it opened its oil and gas markets to outside investment in 1998. Most are with European companies.

[23] David Ignatius, 'The Great Game Gets Rough', *Washington Post*, 26 January 2000, p. A23.

[24] Ed Chow, talk at the Carnegie Endowment for International Peace, Washington DC, 13 March 2001.

Chapter Two

[1] There are several contested names for this territory, part of which includes what is commonly known as Nagorno, or mountainous, Karabakh. The Azeris call it Daghlig or Yukari Garabagh; the Armenians call it Artsakh, or more formally the Lernayin Gharabaghi Hanrapetutyun. The capital is commonly called Stepanakert by Armenians, and Hankenti by Azeris. Thomas Goltz, *Azerbaijan Diary: A Rogue Reporter's Adventures in an Oil-Rich, War-Torn, Post-Soviet Republic* (Armonk, NY and London: M. E. Sharpe, 1998), pp. 87–88.

[2] Michael P. Croissant, *The Armenia–Azerbaijan Conflict: Causes and Implications* (Westport, CT and London: Praeger, 1998), pp. 19–20. On how the situation came about, see W. E. D. Allen and Paul Muratoff, *Caucasian Battlefields* (Cambridge: Cambridge University Press, 1953), pp. 478–500; and Firuz Kazemzadeh, *The Struggle for Transcaucasia* (Oxford: Oxford University Press, 1951), pp. 124–27.

[3] Herzig, *The New Caucasus*, p. 66.

[4] The assassins included a journalist once connected to the nationalist Dashnak party and two of his relatives. Other recent high-profile murder victims include: State Security Committee chief Maj-Gen Marius Yuzbashian; Director-General of Railways Hambartsum Kandilian; President of the Chamber of Industry and Trade Ashot Sarkisian; Mayor of Yerevan Hambartsum Galstian; Prosecutor-General Henrik Khachatrian; and Deputy Defence Minister Vahram Khorkhoruni.

[5] No country has accorded Karabakh official state recognition.

[6] Liz Fuller, 'Attack on Karabakh President Exacerbates Political Tensions in Yerevan', *RFE/RL Newsline*, vol. 4, no. 66, Part I, 3 April 2000.

7 This has not been the case in Azerbaijan, where the military is subordinate to the political leadership since the exile of Surat Husseinov, who led a revolt that eventually drove Elchibey from power and ushered in Aliev. The current defence minister, Safar Abiev, confines his extra-curricular activities to the economic realm. Compare Richard Giragosian, 'Armenian Politics in Uniform', *RFE/RL Newsline*, vol. 3, no. 240, Part I, 13 December 1999.

8 The states in question included Belarus, Czechoslovakia, France, Germany, Italy, Russia, Sweden, Turkey and the US. Karabakh Armenians were not recognised at the conference as representatives of a sovereign state.

9 The origins and chequered history of the Minsk Group are summarised in John J. Maresca, 'The International Community and the Conflict over Nagorno-Karabakh', in Bruce W. Jentleson (ed.) *Opportunities Missed, Opportunities Seized: Preventive Diplomacy in the Post-Cold War World* (Lanham, MD: Rowman and Littlefield, 2000), pp. 68–90.

10 This did not rule out a controversial unofficial proposal for an exchange of territory, whereby Armenia would be allowed to keep the strategic Lachin corridor that connects Karabakh to Armenia in return for the creation of a strategic corridor in Meghri to connect Nakhichevan with Azerbaijan proper.

11 Herzig, *The New Caucasus*, pp. 70–77.

12 Sergiu Celac, 'The Nagorno Karabakh Question: An Update', paper presented at the conference 'The Future of the Caucasus after the Second Chechnya Conflict', Centre for European Policy Studies, Brussels, 27–28 January 2000.

13 'Harbingers of Armenian–Turkish Normalization', *Jamestown Monitor*, vol. 6, no. 19, 27 January 2000; and Sanobar Shermatova, 'Aliyev's Sweet Pill', *Moscow News*, 16 February 2000.

14 'Azeri President's Patience With Russia Has Run Out', *Zerkalo* (Baku), reported in *BBC Worldwide Monitoring*, SU/3744 F/1-2, 22 January 2000; and 'Independence or Unity With Armenia the Only Options for Karabakh', *Snark*, reported in *BBC Worldwide Monitoring*, SU/3766 F/8-9, 17 February 2000.

15 Personal communication, Yousif Aleskerli, August 2000.

16 During the second Chechen war, the oil pipeline from Baku to Novorossiisk ceased to operate before the onset of hostilities in anticipation of attack.

17 Quoted in Zaal Anjaparidze, 'What Post-Yeltsin Russia Promises Georgia?', *Jamestown Foundation Prism*, vol. 6, Part 4, March 2000.

18 Cable from Secretary of State to US Embassy, Baku, 091870, 15 May 1997.

19 *Reuters*, 26 September 2000.

20 Goltz, *Azerbaijan Diary*, pp. 352–92. See also the controversial report 'BP Accused of Backing "Arms for Oil" Coup', *Sunday Times*, 26 March 2000; and Elchibey's response, 'Elchibey: Russia, Armenia and Iran Overthrew Me', *Turkish Daily News*, 6 April 2000.

21 'Kocharian in Georgia Puts "Complementarity" into Practice', *Jamestown Monitor*, vol. 6, no. 67, 4 April 2000.

22 Personal communication, Tom de Waal, May 2000.

23 Daniel Muller, 'The Kurds of Soviet Azerbaijan, 1920–21: New Reconstruction of a Controversial Story', *Central Asian Survey*, vol. 19, no. 1, March 2000, pp. 41–77.

24 This rationale was reported to underlie Turkish Foreign Minister Ismail Cem's February 2001 visit to Iran.

25 David I. Hoffman, 'Oil and Development in Post-Soviet Azerbaijan', *NBR Analysis*, vol. 10, no. 3, August 1999, pp. 25–26.

26 This is according to a planning document of the Turkish General Staff. Personal communication, Gareth Jenkins, February 2000.

27 Patricia Carley, 'Turkey and Central Asia: Reality Comes Calling', in Alvin Z. Rubinstein and Oles M. Smolansky, *Regional Power Rivalries in the New Eurasia* (Armonk, NY and London: M. E. Sharpe, 1995), p. 192. One pretext that has been mentioned frequently in Azerbaijan is the 1921 Kars Treaty between Turkey and the Soviet Union, which may provide a rationale for intervention. The treaty granted Nakhichevan autonomous status under the rule of Azerbaijan, and pledged the signatories to defend the entire region against outside aggression. Views differ, however, on whether the treaty is applicable today, and whether it is considered relevant by Turkish officials. The climate at the time of the Alexandropol, Kars and Moscow treaties is summarised in Richard G. Hovannisian, *The Republic of Armenia (Vol. IV) Between Crescent and Sickle: Partition and Sovietization* (Berkeley, CA: University of California Press, 1996), pp. 390–403.

28 Abdollah Ramezanzadeh, 'Iran's Role as Mediator in the Nagorno-Karabakh Crisis', in Bruno Coppieters (ed.), *Contested Borders in the Caucasus* (Brussels: VUB University Press, 1996), pp. 170–71.

29 Personal communication, Isa Gambar, Baku, May 1997 and Washington DC, March 1999.

30 A 1998 poll conducted for the US Information Agency by SIAR-Baku and the Sociological Research Center of the Armenian Academy of Sciences found that only 12% of Azeri respondents 'had confidence' in Iran to 'deal responsibly with the problems in the Caucasus region'. In Armenia, the response was also 12%. 'Nations of the Caucasus Take Divergent Paths', *USIA Opinion Analysis*, Washington DC, 24 May 1999. According to a February 1999 poll by the firm ARG-Caspian Energy, only 3% of Azerbaijanis consider Iran to be a 'friend', while 9.5% agree that relations should be improved. *RFE/RL Newsline*, vol. 4, no. 33, Part I, 16 February 2000.

31 Elchibey was known to be hostile to Iran, and was often called a Zionist in the Iranian press. See Goltz, *Azerbaijan Diary*, p. 228; Steve Rodan, 'Israel in High-Level Bid for Azerbaijani Projects', *Jane's Defence Weekly*, 22 December 1999, p. 20.

32 Goltz, *Azerbaijan Diary*, p. 164.

33 'Parris: Gesture to Iran Won't Hurt Baku–Ceyhan', *Turkish Daily News*, 21 March 2000.

34 These include many ideologues in Azerbaijan, including former senior adviser Vafa Guluzade, who in August 2000 proposed that Azerbaijan join with Turkey. See also Tadeusz Swietochowski, *Russia and Azerbaijan: A*

Borderland in Transition (New York: Columbia University Press, 1995), pp. 234–35; Herzig, *The New Caucasus*, p. 60; Philip Robins, 'The Middle East and Central Asia', in Peter Ferdinand (ed.), *The New States of Central Asia and Their Neighbours* (London: Royal Institute of International Affairs, 1994), pp. 61–65, 68–70.

[35] Hoffman, 'Oil and Development in Post-Soviet Azerbaijan', p. 21.

Chapter Three

[1] Nancy Lubin, Keith Martin and Barnett Rubin, *Calming the Ferghana Valley: Development and Dialogue in the Heart of Central Asia* (New York: Century Foundation Press, 1999), pp. 34–38.

[2] The homeland of the Meshketian Turks lies in what is today called Javakhetia, a largely Armenian-populated area of southern Georgia along the Turkish and Armenian borders. Almost all have re-emigrated to this region following the 1989 events, which has led to new tensions with the Armenian population. See Aybegul Baydar Aydyngun, 'A Deported Nationality: The Ahiska Turks', *Turkistan Newsletter*, 1 April 1999.

[3] 'Troubles in Fergana', *Central Asia Monitor*, no. 1, 1998.

[4] Bruce Pannier, 'Uzbekistan: Wahhabis – Fundamentalists of the Fergana Valley', *RFE/RL Newsline*, 23 December 1997; and Tamara Makarenko, 'A View on Wahhabism in Uzbekistan', *Turkistan Newsletter*, 27 January 1999.

[5] Now living in exile in Tashkent, Abdullojanov is said to be the richest man in Central Asia through his vast empire of car dealerships and other businesses. He remains active in supporting the Khujandis, but has remained unclear about his own ambitions and whether he seeks to return to Tajik politics. Remarks at seminar 'Conflict and Peace-Building in Tajikistan: A Roundtable with Abdulmalik Abdullojonov', Carnegie Commission on Preventing Deadly Conflict and the Center for Political and Strategic Studies, Washington DC, 15 September 1997.

[6] 'Tajikistan, Still Fighting', *The Economist*, 23 August 1997, pp. 32–33.

[7] Bruce Pannier, 'Puzzling Out the Islamic Movement of Uzbekistan: A View from Kyrgyzstan', *Turkistan Newsletter*, 16 February 2000.

[8] Karimov once said of Akaev, 'all he can do is grin stupidly but does nothing for his people'. The implication was that Uzbekistan should be left to deal with its own wayward militants in its own, preferred way, stated by Karimov as 'shooting them through the head myself'. Nick Megoran, 'The Borders of Eternal Friendship: Krygyz–Uzbek Relations in 1999', *EurasiaNet*, 14 December 1999.

[9] Military assistance has been complicated, however, by the proportionately large influence of non-Ministry of Defence forces in each country, particularly MVD troops such as those under the occasional direction of Tajik warlord Suhrob Qosimov.

[10] Olga Dzyubenko, 'Central Asian States Plan to "Annihilate" Rebels', *Reuters*, 15 August 2000.

[11] 'Islamic "Guerrillas" Training in Kazakhstan', Voice of the Islamic

Republic of Iran, *BBC Worldwide Monitoring*, 15 January 2000; and 'Police Detain 50 "Suspect" Pakistanis', Kazak Kabar television, *BBC Summary of World Broadcasts*, SU/3671 G/2, 21 October 1999.

12 'Kazakhs Anxious over Uzbek Plans for Disputed Border Areas', Kazak television, *BBC Summary of World Broadcasts*, SU/3803 G/3, 31 March 2000; and 'Concern over Unilateral Border Demarcation by Uzbekistan', Tajik television, *BBC Summary of World Broadcasts*, SU/3680 G/2, 1 November 1999.

13 Megoran, 'The Borders of Eternal Friendship'; and interviews with Tajik officials, Dushanbe, June 1998.

14 'Kyrgyzstan and Tajikistan To Build Major Road to Bypass Uzbekistan', *BBC Worldwide Monitoring*, 7 March 2000; 'Building of Highway to China To Be Speeded Up', Asia-Plus, Tajikistan, *BBC Summary of World Broadcasts*, SUW/0616 WE/5, 26 November 1999.

15 Interviews, Bishkek, Khujand and Dushanbe, June 1998.

16 Lubin *et al.*, *Calming the Ferghana Valley*, p. 71. Drug confiscation in Tajikistan alone has increased ten-fold since 1994; 'Drug-Trafficking Increases Tenfold Over Five Years', AsiaPlus, Tajikistan, *BBC Summary of World Broadcasts*, SU/3665 G/2, 14 October 1999. The principal route for opium traffic has been from Khorog (the capital of Gorno-Badakshan) to Murghob and then to Osh and Bishkek, or by way of Andijon, and is commonly known as the 'opium river'. Lowell Bezanis, 'An Enlarged Golden Crescent', *Transitions*, vol. 2, no.19, 20 September 1996. This

route may have been eclipsed by others via Gharm, Kulob and Dushanbe itself.

17 'Iran To Step Up Contacts with Tajik Parliament', Tajik Radio, *BBC Worldwide Monitoring*, 1 April 2000.

18 Nasser to Miles Copeland, quoted in Gore Vidal, 'Nasser's Egypt', *Esquire*, October 1963.

19 'China To Invest $8.45 Billion in Xinjiang', *Reuters*, 19 January 2000.

20 Jonathan N. Lipman, 'Hyphenated Chinese: Sino-Muslim Identity in Modern China', in Gail Hershatter, Emily Honig, Jonathan N. Lipman and Randall Stross (eds), *Remapping China: Fissures in Historical Terrain* (Stanford, CA: Stanford University Press, 1996), pp. 108–10.

21 John Pomfret, 'Separatists Defy Chinese Crackdown: Persistent Islamic Movement May Have Help from Abroad', *Washington Post*, 26 January 2000.

22 Interviews with Zhang Zhou, Vice-Governor of Xinjiang, Urumqi; and Zhao Chang Qing, Chinese Academy of Social Science, Beijing, June 1998.

23 'Assassination [of Nigmatulla Bazakov, leader of the Uighur community in Kyrgyzstan] signals Central Asian Cooperation with China', *Turkistan Newsletter*, 31 March 2000; and Paul Eckert, 'Focus – China, Kazakh Pledge To Fight Separatism', *Reuters*, 24 November 1999.

24 Former Foreign Minister Qian Qichen, quoted in 'Uzbek–Chinese Relations', *RFE/RL Newsline*, 27 December 1997. For a summary of the Shanghai Five meetings, see Mark Burles, *Chinese Policy Toward Russia and*

the Central Asian Republics (Santa
Monica, CA: RAND, Project Air
Force, 1999), pp. 6–8.

25 Vladimir Mukhin, 'Karimov Has
Resurrected the Silk Road: So Far
Russia Is Losing the Competition
with China for Influence in the
Region', *Nezavisimaya Gazeta*, 2
September 2000.

26 Personal communication with
General Xiong Guangkai, Beijing,
June 1998; Michael Pillsbury,
*China Debates the Future Security
Environment* (Washington DC:
National Defense University
Press, 2000), pp. 165–67.

27 Interviews with foreign ministry
officials, Bishkek and Tashkent,
June 1998 and Almaty, May 1997;
and 'President Karimov Specifies
Aims of Visit to China', Uzbek
radio, *BBC Summary of World
Broadcasts*, SU/3689 G/1, 11
November 1999. The Kazak
government wanted to ensure
that a majority of workers on the
pipeline would be Kazaks from
Kazakstan.

28 Edmund Herzig, *Iran and the
Former Soviet South* (London:
Royal Institute of International
Affairs, 1995), pp. 54–55.

29 'Kazakhstan and Iran To Increase
Trade Turnover', Interfax-
Kazakhstan, *BBC Summary of
World Broadcasts*, SU/3662 G/2,
11 October 1999.

30 Interview with Muhammadsharif
Himmatzoda, Chairman, Islamic
Revival Party, Dushanbe, June
1998.

31 Olivier Roy, *The Foreign Policy of
the Central Asian Islamic
Renaissance Party* (New York:
Council on Foreign Relations,
2000), p. 7.

32 Interview with US government
officials, August 1999; and
Makarenko, 'A View on
Wahhabism in Uzbekistan'.

33 Dzyubenko, 'Central Asian States
Plan to "Annihilate" Rebels'.

34 *RFE/RL Newsline*, vol. 4, no. 65,
Part I, 30 March 2000. See also
'Defence Minister Sergeyev
Warns against "Extremists" in
Central Asia', RIA, *BBC Summary
of World Broadcasts*, SU/3803 B/3,
21 March 2000.

35 Interview with Colonel
Adbusattar Karimkulov,
Tashkent, May 1997.

36 'Uzbek–Russian Positions
Coincide, Karimov Tells Putin',
Uzbek television, *BBC Summary
of World Broadcasts*, SU/3717 G/1,
14 December 1999; and
'Uzbekistan Can Rely on Russia
in Fight against Terrorism',
Uzbek television, *BBC Summary
of World Broadcasts*, SU/3746 G/2,
23 January 2000.

37 'Russia To Set Up Military Base
in Tajikistan', *Agence-France Press*,
7 April 1999. The division is
really the native Soviet
formation, and never 'left'
Tajikistan. See Sergei Gretsky,
'Russia and Tajikistan', in
Rubinstein and Smolansky,
*Regional Power Rivalries in the New
Eurasia*, pp. 238–39.

38 Roy, *The Foreign Policy of the
Central Asian Islamic Renaissance
Party*, p. 26.

Chapter Four

1 See Vartan Gregorian, *The
Emergence of Modern Afghanistan:
Politics of Reform and
Modernization 1880–1946*
(Stanford, CA: Stanford
University Press, 1969).

2 Mahnaz Z. Ispahani, *Roads and
Rivals: The Politics of Access in the
Borderlands of Asia* (London: I. B.
Tauris, 1989), pp. 1–14, 27–30.

3 Afghanistan's population is

estimated to be roughly 41% Pushtun, 16% Tajik, 15% Hazara, 11% Uzbek and 17% others, such as Baluch and Turkmen.

4 Larry P. Goodson, 'Periodicity and Intensity in the Afghan War', *Central Asian Survey*, vol. 17, no. 3, September 1998, pp. 481–82; and Barnett R. Rubin, *The Search for Peace in Afghanistan: From Buffer State to Failed State* (New Haven, CT and London: Yale University Press, 1995), p. 124.

5 Barnett R. Rubin, *The Fragmentation of Afghanistan: State Formation and Collapse in the International System* (New Haven, CT and London: Yale University Press, 1995), p. 179; Anthony Arnold, *Afghanistan: The Soviet Invasion in Perspective* (Stanford, CA: Hoover Institution Press, 1985), p. 118.

6 For details of the complex motivations of each, as well as Iran, during this period, see Rubin, *The Search for Peace in Afghanistan*, pp. 103–17.

7 Zalmay Khalilzad, *Prospects for the Afghan Interim Government* (Santa Monica, CA: RAND Corporation, 1991), pp. 10–16; and Rubin, *The Search for Peace in Afghanistan*, pp. 112–24.

8 Personal communication with General Naseerullah Babar, Islamabad, June 1998; Ahmed Rashid, *Taliban, Islam, Oil and the New Great Game in Central Asia* (London: I. B. Tauris, 2000), p. 26.

9 'Afghan Factions Fight in North', *Associated Press*, 2 August 2000; and Kate Clark, 'Opposition Forces Press Taliban', *BBC News Online*, 17 August 2000.

10 Arkady Dubnov, 'Moscow Appears To Have Come to the Conclusion that It Must Work with the Taliban', Institute for War and Peace Reporting, 21 September 2000; 'France Edging toward Recognizing Afghanistan's Taliban Government', *Stratfor.com's Global Intelligence Update*, 20 September 2000.

11 Citha D. Maass, 'The Afghanistan Conflict: External Involvement', *Central Asian Survey*, vol. 18, no. 1, March 1999, pp. 65–66.

12 See Anthony Hyman, *Afghanistan under Soviet Domination, 1964–91* (London: Macmillan, 1992), pp. 46–47, 69–70.

13 See Vali Nasr, *International Relations of an Islamist Movement: The Case of the Jama'at-i Islami of Pakistan* (New York: Council on Foreign Relations, 2000), pp. 28–29; and Roger Howard, 'Probing the Ties that Bind Militant Islam', *Jane's Intelligence Review*, February 2000.

14 Barry Bearak, 'Adding to Pakistan's Misery, a Heroin Epidemic', *New York Times*, 19 April 2000. Afghanistan's own opium production doubled in 1999, yielding an estimated 4,581 tons, the world's highest. See Pierre-Arnaud Chouvy, 'Taliban's Drug Dilemma: Opium Production vs. International Recognition', *The Analyst*, 8 December 1999.

15 Robert D. Kaplan, 'The Lawless Frontier', *Atlantic Monthly*, September 2000.

16 Interview with Iftekhar Murshed, Additional Secretary, Afghanistan, Ministry of Foreign Affairs, Islamabad, June 1998.

17 See Rashid, *Taliban, Islam, Oil and the New Great Game*, pp. 157–82.

18 For the pivotal role of Baluch nationalism in Pakistan, see Selig Harrison, *In Afghanistan's Shadow: Baluch Nationalism and Soviet Temptations* (New York and Washington DC: Carnegie Endowment for International

Peace, 1981), pp. 71–91; and Ispahani, *Pakistan: Dimensions of Insecurity*, pp. 25–26.

[19] The Ghilzais are known to have a historic though long-suppressed pro-Ottoman tendency, which dates back even further to their alleged Turkic origins. Durranis, on the other hand, tend to be viewed as Persianised interlopers. See Rahimullah Yusufzai, 'Influence of Durrani–Ghalji (Ghilzai) Rivalry on Afghan Politics', *Regional Studies* (Islamabad), Autumn 1983, reprinted in *Afghanistan: Past, Present and Future* (Islamabad: Institute for Regional Studies, 1997), pp. 76–121.

[20] See Graham E. Fuller and Rend Rahim Francke, 'Is Shi'ism Radical?', *Middle East Quarterly*, vol. 7, no. 1, March 2000, pp. 11–20; and Mahnaz Ispahani, 'The Perils of Pakistan', *New Republic*, 16 March 1987, pp. 20–21.

[21] Harrison, *In Afghanistan's Shadow*, p. 97.

[22] Personal communication with Uzbek Foreign Ministry official, Tashkent, June 1998.

[23] Guy Dinmore, 'Iranian Gas Exploitation May Include India Pipeline', *Financial Times*, 23 April 2000.

[24] Personal communication with Major-General K. Sudhakar, Indian Army, July 1998; Jaswant Singh, *Defending India* (London: Macmillan, 1999), pp. 110–11, 162–72, 239–47, 278–85. In 1999, India announced its intention to raise an entirely new army corps based in Ladakh, and later issued its largest-ever increase in defence expenditure.

[25] See Hooman Peimani, 'Afghanistan Engagement', *South China Morning Post*, 16 February 2000.

[26] See, for example, Rashid, *Taliban*,

Islam, Oil and the New Great Game.

[27] P. Stobdan, 'The Afghan Conflict and Regional Security', *Strategic Analysis*, August 1999, pp. 719–47; interview with Rafik Saifullin, Deputy Director, Institute for Strategic and Regional Studies, Tashkent, June 1998.

[28] Kanai Manayev, 'Interview with Satorzoda Abdunabi (Deputy Foreign Minister of Tajikistan)', *Times of Central Asia*, 21 December 2000.

[29] *Slovo Kyrgyzstana*, Bishkek, 16 June 2000.

[30] Carol Saivetz, 'Putin Is Not an Arabist', *Gulf 2000* discussion list, 2 June 2000 (cited with author's permission).

[31] Rubin, *The Search for Peace in Afghanistan*, p. 25.

[32] Robert Byron, *The Road to Oxiana* (London: Picador, 1981 (first published 1937)), pp. 246–47.

Conclusion

[1] Niall Ferguson, *The Pity of War* (London: Penguin, 1999), p. 80. The author refers to the intemperance of a weak power (Germany) and the negligence of a strong one (Britain) during the run-up to the First World War.

[2] See Sir Michael Howard, 'The World According to Henry; from Metternich to Me', review of Henry Kissinger's *Diplomacy*, *Foreign Affairs*, vol. 73, no. 3, May–June 1994.

[3] Brzezinski, *The Grand Chessboard*, p. 40.

[4] The failure to agree on what constituted reciprocity (that is, mutual restraint) led to the collapse of multi-power diplomacy on Afghanistan. Rubin, *The Search for Peace in Afghanistan*, pp. 84ff.